Just a little prick

This is a term some nurses and doctors use when giving an injection. I am pleased to say I have never used this term, over a period when I must have given thousands of injections. This may have been a fear of the patient saying "I know what you are but what are going to do?"

For Deborah,

Siempre Tujo

Table of contents

Chapter One: Early life

Forgive the first chapter which; is about my early years however, I think important to show from whence I came.

I was a war baby. Born of humble, hardworking parents, the 3rd boy and then I had a sister. Rumour has it my Mum wanted to throw me in the river as she really wanted a girl!! We resided in a very small village about 5 miles from Boston, Lincolnshire where the bus service ran once a week into town (if you were lucky). Until you could afford a bicycle you walked everywhere. If anyone saw a car it was talked about for days however, the grocer van came once a week and he fortunately sold almost everything including the old acid batteries to keep the radio going which; was the sole entertainment other than what you made amongst yourselves. We had no electricity or gas at that time and relied on coal fires for warmth and primus lamps which ran on paraffin (also supplied by the visiting grocer) The secret for my Mum was not to forget anything as it was a long walk or bike ride for one of us if she did. Being resourceful country folk we were as self sufficient as possible i.e. home grown vegetables, keeping a pig and some chickens. It was an annual event when it came time to kill the pig we had nurtured for a year. Everyone was involved in preparing for the event and when the deed was done; my job was to go around the village on my bike to deliver the fresh produce e.g. sausages, fry and haslets. I still don't really know why this ritual was carried out as the next day someone from the other side of the village would arrive with same type of produce which; they had prepared the day before.

One of my first memories of self-sufficiency was often talked about by my Mum and one of survival over adversity and the rich farmers who by and large had a good life at that time. The story goes that the farmer had a mother turkey and seven young ones. Every day this brood travelled from the farm to our house and proceeded to raid the vegetable garden. My mother waited and waited until the young turkeys grew. When the time was right she asked me to keep watch and give her the nod. The brood eventually came into vision and proceed to the veggie patch, as they came around the side of the house Mum counted to six and then grabbed the seventh. Unfortunately, she then had no idea what to do though between us we managed to hold the thing down and with a mighty blow with an axe she managed to decapitate the bird. When my Dad came home he remarked that something smelled rather good, yes Christmas came early that year. Unfortunately, the brood never did return.

Although we were not very 'well off' a lot of pride was held in the way we lived and what my parents worked very hard for; there was always plenty of food on the table mostly made from the fresh produced from the garden. Of course, this was at the time of post war rationing. I really don't know how not only my Mum, but other families managed with the core ingredients required. My Mum also worked and yet still produced meals everyday for a relatively large family.

One seemingly austere measure when meat or main course ingredients were lacking was that we would be given 'pudding' first so we would not miss too much of a main course. This was usually a steamed pudding of some sort, my favourites were always spotted dick or treacle with homemade custard as we usually had plenty of eggs however, and sugar was rationed so sometimes it was not too sweet!

Pride was maintained not only in the vegetable garden but the flower garden which was surrounded by a hedge to separate from the neighbours. I recall the hedge was maintained by us and the neighbour and was becoming damaged. After a while it was evident the postman was breaking through as a short cut. We did not have a flush toilet and the "dilly cart" came round once a week to empty the bucket from the outside loo. The answer to the hedge problem was that mum and the neighbour dug a hole at the bottom of the hedge and filled it with two buckets of effluent and sure enough the postman took his shortcut once too often and went up to his knees in the hole. The hedge survived and indeed thrived with the extra fertilizer!!! But the postman went the long way round henceforth.

1st day at junior school

The primary school was about a 2 mile walk, (longer if you went on the road all the way) so we used to take a short cut through a farm which backed on to the school. This was not only a short cut but quicker if you were unlucky and got chased by the resident geese. I was not very big with short legs, not a fast runner so consequently often got bitten on the arse by these mad bloody geese,

I always remember junior school as a happy time. It was run by a husband and wife who made the learning enjoyable.

Secondary school was about 8 miles away and we had to go by bus.

I remember the first day I was confronted by the class bully (who was a friend of the head boy) he was teasing me for being small. I retaliated by knocking him on his arse and giving him a bloody nose. My dad had taught me well, Head boy reported this inaccurately saying that I was the aggressor.

Physical education classes were joined by streaming groups i.e. 1a joined 2a so inevitably 2a group were a year older and bigger.

My first PE lesson the teacher chose me as he had heard of the previous fracas, to enter the man made boxing ring to face a big lad in my own stream (1a) within 1 round I knocked ten barrels of shit out of him. I was then confronted by the biggest kid from 2a who promptly did the same to me. Lesson learned 'do not get in a fight unless you think you can win

During the summer holidays we were expected to work on the local farms, money earned was for spends on the days out to the seaside and most of all to supplement buying football kit or any other little extras required for next term at school.

This could be picking potatoes, heading tulips or daffodils which was back breaking. One of the best jobs I had was during the harvest. The local policeman used to take his annual leave to allow him to earn some cash as coppers were not paid well. Our village copper was a big guy with ginger hair and an enormous ginger moustache. He was known as a no nonsense but fair man, well respected. My job was to drive the tractor pulling the hay cart. All I had to do was let the clutch in or out to stop and go (one of the workers would put it in gear for me) PC ginger was on the top of the cart stacking the bails of straw which had been passed up to him. After a while this got a bit boring and made my leg ache, so I decided to put the gear leaver in neutral unfortunately I put it in second gear instead and let the clutch out too quickly. Tractor and trailer shot forward quite suddenly and PC ginger fell of the cart. I have never ran so fast in my life but was forgiven when he caught me and everyone had a good laugh.

In spite of the hardships my parents managed to buy a full set of the Encyclopaedia Britannica, this was a source of great enjoyment to be able to read about the world as it was then. One thing that remained in my mind forever was a picture of the Colosseum and one of the statue of Romulus and Remus suckling the wolf in Rome. Many years later on our first visit to Rome and the first time I saw the colosseum, the hair on the back of my neck tingled and did so for about a week, I still get excited most days by seeing live pictures from live web-cams.

When I was 12 yrs., my dad had recently had an accident on his motor bike and was quite seriously ill. When he was fully recovered, we all moved nearer to Boston. Dad progressed to owning his first car which broadened horizons for social activities, holidays etc.

Being nearer to town meant it was easier to go to support Boston United FC amongst other things. BUFC even played Spurs at White Hart Lane in the FA cup but lost. At this time I joined the St Johns ambulance brigade which; I think started me on an ambition to work in the care sector. I rose to rank of sergeant and captained the team in achieving Lincolnshire and Midlands champions only missing out on the national champions by 1 point.

Even in those days it was standard practice for local events to have a first aider on site. For this reason we got free entry into the cinema, football matches, shows etc.

Highlight of the year was the annual camping trip for 1 week. We were joined by all the cadets in Lincolnshire, a really good opportunity to meet new people. Enjoyable times were had in Skegness or the Norfolk coast.

Chapter Two: First jobs

1st Job

On leaving school my first job was in a workwear shop in town. The manager was a right miserable git who I think was miffed because he didn't work in the company smart gentleman's wear in the high street. I was not allowed to interact with the customers. The other assistant was a good guy. One day when the manager had gone for lunch and the other assistant was serving a customer; a chap came in to buy a pair of Wellington boots and he was in a hurry. I showed him the range and he made a purchase. On the managers return the assistant told him that he had been busy and that I had sold this chap a pair of wellies. The assistant was bollocked rigid for allowing me to serve and I was told I would be leaving the following Saturday. The next day I had got myself a new job and took great delight in telling him to stick his job and promptly walked out.

 2nd job was in a canning factory where I worked mainly in research and experimental work in making sauces e.g. tomato sauce for the baked beans.

The other part of the job was on the production line, making the large batches of syrup/sauce which went down a series of pipes to fill the cans of peas, beans etc. During the summer season we made sugar rich sauces for fresh fruit e.g. strawberries, gooseberries and raspberries. This attracted thousands of wasps who imbibed large amounts of the syrup that contained food dye, they inevitably became extremely fat and instead of being black/yellow they changed to black/red. They were always sleepy and this enabled me to indulge in my favourite trick of tying a thin piece of string around their waist and when they woke would fly around on the end of the string like a live balloon.

At this time I smoked cigarettes but not many in fact during the football season I stopped and restarted when the season finished (completely daft)

Every Friday afternoon a guy used to come to the syrup room for his cup of tea, he always offered me a 'Park Drive'. Looking back this is when I knew I was addicted to ciggies as I really looked forward to Friday afternoons and Jack's Park Drive. It was nearly 60 years before I was able to kick the habit.

Chapter Three Start of nursing career. Cadet scheme.

On my 17th birthday I commenced work at Bracebridge Heath Hospital (later to become St. Johns Hospital) this was a big adventure as it was 35 miles from home and a psychiatric hospital, and to be honest I had no idea what to expect.

There were 3 of us doing the cadet nursing course as a pilot for future recruitment. Two of us went on to achieve qualification and a career plan. This pre-nursing course was for 1 year until we reached 18 yrs. of age and comprised of 3 months experience in 4 areas of the hospital that normal students did not get. We also attended college to gain further education qualifications.

My first allocation was to the occupational therapy department which was a most enjoyable experience with both instructors being very knowledgeable and skilful. This was my first experience of meeting patients, I remember it being rather daunting and a somewhat frightening one. Remember, this was 1958 and all the wards had locked doors at all times, though patients were allowed to go out if their condition was stable. I recall one patient continually talked to himself and 'others' rather loudly and another patient had put up with for too long, it took 3 of us to prevent him nailing the noisy persons tongue to the store cupboard door.

The OT department was on the 1st floor and one day one of the instructors took me up to the 2nd floor to show me where all the belongings of Polish (from 2nd world war) patients were stored, the room was about 40 feet square and stacked to the ceiling with suit cases full of all sorts of valuables e.g. watches, gold chains, clocks and clothing. Many years later I went back and all of this stuff had disappeared but I could never find out where it went.

Second allocation was to the pharmacy department where I learned a lot about medicines and how they were used. Of special note was the chief pharmacist who was involved in all sorts of scams e.g. selling condoms amongst other things. He also kept a herd of pigs and he use to collect all the waste food from the wards and kitchen in special 50 gallon containers to feed his herd. I don't think he expected that drugs (mainly antibiotics) would end up in the food chain, but I am sure it could be one of the reasons why this happened.

Third allocation was in the stores where nothing unusual happened except I learned how to file invoices and weigh out a kilo of sugar!!!! A lot of time was spent playing table tennis or snooker in the staff games room.

Fourth allocation was the laboratory, x-ray dept. and dental surgery assisting the dentist on his visits which occurred about once a month. Again a lot of time honing the table tennis and snooker skills.

As I was not allowed to 'live in' until I was 18 years old meant during the time I was a cadet I lodged with my cousin about 4 miles from work and I cycled to work which kept me fit. When the weather was good I would bike home to Boston at weekends as opposed to getting the bus or train.

I remember I was paid £3. 10 (£3. 50p) shillings a week and paid out £1. 10 shillings (£1.50p) for board and lodge. The remaining £2 was for having a good time and savings!!!!

Chapter Four 'Living in' and my first wards

At 18yrs of age I was allowed to live in the nurses' home, this was segregated with locked doors between male and female. Not only were the doors locked but originally had 4 x 6 inch screws securing them however; the screws had been removed and the heads sawn off and pushed back into the holes. A master key was kept in the laundry room for any visiting needs.

All meals had to be taken in the restaurant in the main hospital building however, there was a facility to make small meals and ingredients could be obtained from the kitchen. We had to do our own clothes washing and ironing. The doors were locked at midnight by the night superintendent. An alarm clock was not needed as the superintendent would make it part of his last round to wake everyone on early shift who had left a card on the door to their room. One lad complained that he had not been given a wakeup call, the next morning we were all woken by the superintendent kicking a dustbin down the corridors, nobody ever complained again.

My first ward was in a 70 bed ward separate from the main building, it also had 10 beds on a veranda for patients who had or were recovering from tuberculosis.

It overlooked the main sports fields i.e. football pitch, cricket pitch and Bowling Green. These were some of the best sporting facilities in the county as they were well maintained by dedicated groundsmen and of cause cheap labour by the use of patients as part of their treatment.

My first day trying to create an impression was to be 10 minutes early for my shift, only to be met by the charge nurse saying "you're late" when I questioned this he informed me that as I was resident I had to be on duty 15 minutes early to allow for me to take my evening meal in the canteen.

Even though my first meeting with him was rather brusque he eventually became a world of knowledge and a good mentor. His pride and joy was the office desk which I now know that he had a certain amount of OCD though at the time was not recognised as such. Apparently someone kept removing items from the desk. On one occasion I reached for the eraser and it could be not moved , on closer inspection it had a hole through the centre with a piece of string through, this had been threaded through a hole drilled in the desk and the string was tied to a house brick. To use the eraser you had to pull the string up and hold it preventing the brick from falling whilst trying to use the eraser with one hand.

The staff nurse offered to teach me how to administer the medicines. This consisted of him going to the medicine cupboard where most of the tablets were stored in containers with up to 500 tablets in each (clearly labelled) the staff nurse emptied a few tablets from each container and put them all together in his white coat pocket. He then proceeded to go around the ward, giving out the appropriate tablets to each. On one occasion he offered one patient a tablet and promptly removed it and said "they don't suit you have one of these instead"

Later on in my experience is was always a consideration if you were asked to help on another ward that did you know the drugs (that is without looking at the prescriptions) for speed. The strange thing is I don't recall any major mistakes surprisingly.

On this first ward one of the patient quite often dislocated his jaw when yawning. This meant he had to go to the local general hospital A&E to have it put back in place under anaesthetic. This of cause meant a member of staff had to stay with until he had recovered. One day he came down the ward pointing to his jaw and moaning. Another patient went up to him and said "I'm f---g sick of you doing this" and promptly punched him in the mouth and knocked his jaw back in place. Apparently it did not dislocate ever again!

Chapter Five: Life in the nurses' home.

'Living in' as a student was a happy but hard working time? Like most nurses at that time you had to work for 47.5.hours a week as well as study for your qualification. Self-discipline was essential to enable study time as well as working the long hours though I suppose 3 days off a fortnight was not too bad as sometimes you had a 3 day weekend off. Shifts at that time were 1 week mornings 0700 to 1315 with 1 day off in the week. Weekends were 0700 to 2115 both Saturday and Sunday. All the second week was 1245 to 2115 and weekend off.

We were allowed to work overtime if shifts were free. When I was saving to buy a motorbike I worked 0700 to 2115 for 12 straight days and just had every other weekend off, almost doubling my salary but it was only possible for about 6 weeks and hopefully was due some holiday as we did have 6 weeks per annum.

We still had time for the odd party. One night we were all fairly rat arsed and were having fun with fire hose which got somewhat out of hand. The next morning we were called to the chief's office and given an almighty bollocking. In our defence we said that we knew who had reported us and wished to know why he was at the time exiting the female section of the nurses home fastening his flies and his shirt half removed. . Most of the senior managers including the chief male nurse lived in rather nice Victorian houses in the grounds.

This chap was the supplies officer (very senior) The chief asked that we keep the fire hose for fighting fires in the future and this time we would say no more!

One scary and very sad episode happened in the space of 2 new moons. The first one was an extremely well respected fellow who was an alcoholic and had a drug dependency though we did not know this until later. He had been to the pub and when he got back to his room took some very powerful sleeping pills, forgetting he had taken some before he went out. Ambulance called but he died on the way to hospital. Accidental death. He was in room 8!!

Exactly one full moon later a young student had found his boyfriend who had hanged himself on a golf course in the town where he lived 20 miles away. He came back after his weekend off and was found the next morning having hung himself in one of the hospital out buildings. Verdict suicide. He was in room 9!!

I was in room 10 and changed rooms very quickly.

There were 2 good pubs outside the hospital gates. My mate Derek and I were in having a drink and the landlord asked us if we would be so good as to take one of our Doctors home as he had had too much. (This Dr was a consultant psychiatrist and one of the foremost authorities in his field) unfortunately he was an alcoholic. He was a tall guy and weighed about 17 stone and we were struggling to manage so we found a wheel barrow in someone's front garden into which we placed the good doctor and wheeled him home. After getting him into front door Derek noticed a bottle of whisky sticking out of the Drs' jacket pocket and nicked it thinking he wouldn't know, but the good Dr sought us out the next morning to ask for it back.

As I began to work on the wards I often commented on a certain smell associated with the wards with a high number of patients with schizophrenia, no one was able to explain this though some agreed. (Some years later a female psychiatrist became aware of this and began a research project however she then left the hospital and as far as I am aware her research was not completed.) I think recently this type of research has been rekindled.

One night after a drinking party one of the students was so rat arsed that we had to carry him upstairs and put him on his bed, prior to leaving him to sleep it off, we removed his shoes. I remarked to the other lad "bloody hell I can smell schizophrenia" then went to my room to sleep off my own hangover. Two weeks later this student did not return from weekend off and his mother rang to say he had been admitted to the local mental hospital in Manchester with acute schizophrenia. Co-incidence or what?

Chapter Six January 1960, started nurse training

In January 1960 I started my proper training, the first 3 months was called the PTS (preliminary training school) this was 9-5 and every weekend off, a lot to learn.

We then returned to working on the wards with 1 day a week in the training room.

One of the requirements of the older staff (trained and untrained) was that their previous experience must have been in the armed forces, a good sportsman or could play a musical instrument. There was a plethora of really good sportsmen including some who had played for Yorkshire county cricket team, one played professional football as goalkeeper for Newcastle united. one had been a professional golfer, one a professional boxer. Obviously we had really good teams competing as amateurs throughout the county. This coupled with the exceptional facilities made the hospital a good venue.

My first ward after PTS was always my favourite.

Bath days were always a fun day!! I was asked by the staff nurse to prepare a patient for his bath, this chap was always extremely uncooperative and truculent and would never willingly go for a bath. A fellow student had warned me about this and that the staff always gave new students this guy to work with, without much success. I therefore asked one of nursing assistants if he would be so good as to show me how to deal with this situation. I must say I learned a lot about distraction technique as this chap was undressed in record time.

I worked with many of these assistant nurses, watched and learned about the different ways of working. A much admired members of the ward team.

Bathrooms were quite large with 4 baths in each corner sectioned off by curtains for privacy.

One elderly gentleman who only had a poo once a week, whilst in the bath, when it floated to the top of the water he would scoop it up with his hand and throw it over his shoulder, it invariably would land in one of the adjacent baths, where the recipient would also scoop it out. Every ward had a patient who did all the 'dirty' jobs and this guy would then collect it off the floor and dispose of it. In spite of the jobs he would do, he was one of the happiest soles I have ever met. He had 2 ambitions in life, one was to scrub the ballroom floor and the other was to clean up an incontinent female. I don't think he ever achieved either.

On this ward I had my first experiences of savants. On Saturday afternoon this gentleman would watch the full football results on BBC sports roundup and within 10 minutes could relay the scores of every team in every division. He could also do the square root of any number suggested, even large 6 or 7 figure numbers. Though he could not remember how to get dressed. One other young man who could not even tell you his name and needed help to get dressed, could do a 5000 piece jig saw puzzle in about half an hour. His mum would bring him 2 puzzles of 5000 plus every Sunday afternoon and he would complete them in a couple of hours.

We were having a coffee break when the Doctor came to do his ward round. The charge nurse came out of the office and said the Dr needed to see the patient who had had a fall but would someone clean the blood away before taking him in. One of the staff promptly picked up a used floor cloth and wiped the blood from the guys face. I immediately said "wow, talk about Stone Age nursing" and this term became legend whenever any such procedure lacked finesse or was outdated.

At weekends when we worked from 0700 to 2115 both Saturday and Sunday the routine was we worked very hard on Saturday morning to get all the routine jobs completed. This left all afternoon to watch sport on TV. Sundays also were equally relaxed, as long as the patients every need was met. One Sunday afternoon I needed help with a task and could not find the assistant nurse for about half an hour, eventually finding him fast asleep on the top shelf of the linen cupboard. Four of the wards shared a courtyard for exercise. These were surrounded by a wall about 15 feet high immediately before this was a ditch of about 10 feet deep and 10 feet wide. I think these are called a 'ha-ha' and was designed by the Victorians to prevent anyone getting over the wall but whilst inside the courtyard they could see beyond the wall. (An example of this still exists today in the grounds of the Lawn Complex on Union Road Lincoln), One day we had an extremely violent storm. On receipt of a phone call from a senior nurse to say one of the drains in the courtyard was blocked and water could not drain, one of the assistant nurses was asked to take 2 patients out to unblock it. Duly dispatched and removed the drain cover and probed with a spade revealed a clunk of metal on metal. The nurse asked the patients to hold on while he fetched a wheelbarrow from the garden workshop. On his return he proceeded to remove the blockage and load it into the barrow. When the drain was empty and the wheelbarrow full he took it over to behind the cricket pavilion where there was a hosepipe and proceeded to rinse the contents of the find. This revealed about £300 of half-crowns and 2 shilling pieces which were put into sacks and loaded into the boot of his car. 2 weeks later he came to work in a brand new car!

The ballroom was a wonderful facility which had a stage and all the associated back stage dressing rooms. It also boasted a sprung floor made of oak parquet and a projection room. The annual hospital ball was held in the ballroom was a grand affair to which everyone attended in their finery. No expense was spared, music was provided by the top dance bands of the time. Victor Sylvester orchestra, The Ted Heath orchestra, The Ivy Benson band who was an all-female band, were regular guests.

The ball room was also used for social gatherings of both male and female patients, including regular showing of the latest movies. Strict supervision had to be maintained during these events as they could be unpredictable.

One morning on my way to work I was stopped by a patient who was also on his way to work with other patients on a farm about 20 miles away. This chap had advanced paranoid schizophrenia and was recognised as the fittest, strongest person in the hospital although always said to be a friend of all the staff, though you were taught never to take this for granted. He asked me for some change to by some cigarettes on his way to work. I put my hand in my pocket and pulled out a £5 note (rare to have that much money at all) as it was about half a month's wages. He took it out of my hand saying "that will do". Now, I am not going to argue and thought there goes a fiver. At about 6 o'clock in the evening a knock came on my room door and there stood GG offering a five pound note back and a packet of cigarettes in payment for the loan.

I was helping out on a ward where a newly promoted charge nurse BE was also standing in for annual leave when along comes the Medical Superintendents secretary and after a few minutes in the office with BE who popped his head out of the door and asked if we could look after things and discreetly let him know if anyone important came on the ward. After about half an hour the secretary duly came out of the office somewhat dishevelled and quickly left the ward. BE promptly came out of the office to say "she had not long been married and her husband was not experienced and they wanted to try sex 'doggy fashion' but they didn't know how to do it and would BE show her how? He said she didn't get the hang of it the first time so he had to show her twice.

On the ward I was allocated at the 0time was again standing in for annual leave. This was a very busy ward with most patients bedridden. BE tended to remain in the office a lot, except after morning coffee break when he would disappear to the toilet with a selection of the daily newspapers. The staff toilet was situated in the sluice area. One day we thought we had had enough of this and we would seek revenge. So we made out we were the cleaner tidying up and mopping the floor, in fact we made a cleaner type noises whilst splashing surgical spirit around, particularly under the toilet door. Then set light to it. The door shot open and there was BE with trousers down and stood on the toilet seat with flames around his ankles. We thought that would do the trick and promptly put the fire out before any damage of injury was caused. It could have gone wrong but it didn't.

Next ward experience was the main admission ward and you never knew what was coming through the door. Remember this was before the time when many new drugs were being developed for e.g. tranquilizers, neuroleptics etc. As these became more developed and used more often, even before patients came into hospital the acute type illnesses such as acute mania became less frequent.

Because this type of acute illness brought untold risks of injury to staff, the treatment was strong sedation and then the use of electro-convulsive therapy (ECT) a good many patients with severe symptoms required the use of the padded cell to prevent injury to themselves or staff. Amazingly these patients generally recovered fairly quickly and returned to normal lives.

One such patient who was admitted on a section, with acute schizophrenia had escaped through the smallest of windows. Police and other agencies were alerted as was the practice and he was not seen overnight. The next morning we received a call from the local RAF station enquiring if we had lost a patient. Apparently a pilot went to his Vulcan aeroplane to go on a mission, there sat in the pilot's seat was our patient fast asleep in his pyjamas. We were not sure how he avoided security or even gained access to the plane as the cockpit was quite a climb to get in.

This ward was always a good placement as it was separate from the main hospital and had its own kitchen led by a fabulous cook. The food was always amazing. The work was always interesting as all the 'new' treatments were always used on this ward first.

One of the charge nurses who was very intelligent and highly thought of as a professional carer. When new drugs (tranquilisers etc.) came out he always tried them himself to see what effect they would have. Fortunately he never had any adverse effects. The other shift charge nurse was different altogether but never the less a very astute at patient care. He was always extremely well groomed and conducted himself with 'style' I was therefore most surprised that one day we were having a discussion about a patients treatment when he walked across to the office hand wash sink. Unzipped his flies and peed in the sink. On completion of this task he turned around and carried on the discussion as if this was normal!

On this ward I had to give my first injection, it happened as a patient was needing sedation as he was attacking everyone in an acute mania stage. These situations invariably needed about 6 staff to bring the episode to a satisfactory conclusion. The sedation had been prepared and ready. I was the smallest member of staff and just observing and was told I would be giving the injection. I had only practiced on oranges in the classroom and knew the theory about missing nerves etc., Bearing in mind there were about 6 bodies rolling around on the floor that it was difficult to determine who was who. "Where do I inject" I asked. The reply was "the first bit of bare flesh you see, stick it in" It was so lucky the boss didn't get it stuck in his arse!!!On one other such occasion, a staff nurse announced 'ok lads I have got him' so everyone stood up including the patient whilst on the floor the staff nurse was holding the charge nurse securely by the legs.

Night duty was usually very boring as everyone was asleep and the tendency to sleep yourself was common. Each ward had 1 member of staff to look after about 60 to 70 patients. The secret if you were going to have a kip was not to get caught. So we always slept with our heads close to water pipes. The first person on the night superintendents round set his alarm and the tapping of pipes started in sequence as per the boss's routine rounds. One night we got it wrong and got caught on the third ward. The boss announced that it was like 'bloody Filingdales early warning station'.

One night there had been a patients dance party in the ballroom, the strongest drink allowed was cider. When we went to' dinner' at about 1130, there was some bottles of cider left over and we could help ourselves. So dinner and a litre of cider it was. Went back to the ward and the next thing was a patient waking me up saying "it's time to go home in half an hour"

It is said you always remember where you were when JFK was shot, I was on nights on Fillingham ward watching it all on TV.

Apart from the patients who required a single room for whatever reason the majority of the patients slept in dormitories. One night I am sitting reading, all is quiet when a patient got out of bed and proceeded to the fire bucket and promptly drank almost all the water in it (about 2 gallons!) on returning to and climbing back in to bed he promptly gave a big burp and projectile vomited his stomach contents, unfortunately it spread over about 10 other beds. He got back into bed and went straight to sleep whilst all the other beds had to be changed.

I am not sure whether this is true but I have every reason to believe it is so.when a patient died it was procedure that a trained member of staff went to identify the body in the mortuary when it was collected by the undertaker. On one such occasion a staff nurse went to carry out this task. There was only one body in the mortuary and it was not the one supposedly to be collected by the undertaker. Apparently, there had been 2 patients die within 2-3 days with similar names. One was to be buried in his home town of Grimsby and the other was to be buried in the hospital cemetery as he had no next of kin to take responsibility. 0The hospital burial took place the day before the undertaker came to take the other one back to Grimsby. This was pre 1948 when the Chief Superintendent ruled with a rod of iron, he had to be informed of this. After due consideration he ruled that 2 members of staff and 2 trusted patients would go in the night and dig up the one buried in the hospital cemetery and swap him over with the one from the mortuary. So in effect 1 person had 2 burial services and the other had none!!

As I said at the beginning I am not sure whether to believe this however, one of the staff who had apparently carried out the task told me the story and every once in a while it came up in conversations and the story was always consistent. One of the patients involved was still resident when I worked there, it was noted he always had the very best of everything but would not talk about his involvement.

A regular occurrence was going out to bring back absconders which, could be anywhere in the UK. We often were needed to fetch back a chap who normally resided in Gainsborough who regularly went down to London to lobby his MP. This was often a nice day out as the patient was not very big and easily managed.

I was once asked by a consultant if I would be able to take a private patient back to Sicily. Fortunately I was due a long weekend so got myself prepared, passport, sun protector, shorts etc. All travel arrangements were made. On the day before we were due to go, the patients parents arrived to take him back to Sicily. Bugger!!

A scary one was when we had to fetch 2 psychopaths back from London Bow Street by train. These 2 guys could be dangerous and one was a club bouncer and known as the second hardest case in Scunthorpe. Before setting of we had approval to take some tranquiliser in injection form, along with some antidote to phenothiazine as these 2 guys were on a monthly injection of a tranquilizer which; was supposed to stop them absconding due to the potential side effects which to a certain extent immobilised them. Two of us went and presented to the police station and set a plan, agreed with the desk sergeant. Because of the potential danger to us and in turn the public we had agreed that both would get an injection of sedation. This was promptly done and we left to have some lunch before returning to pick them up and be transferred to Kings Cross station for the journey home. The desk sergeant was eager to know what we had used and where could he get it. The train was absolutely packed with no seats in second class whatsoever. Bearing in mind we were having to hold these two guys up by their trouser belts and walk the full length of the train, difficult on a 3 hour journey. We eventually came to a first class compartment which was empty, so we sat them in this cabin. I found the guard and explained the situation and he gave us permission to travel first class. We then went to the buffet car for a beer!

The rug!!

All wards had two charge nurses to cover each shift. On one ward when one person was in charge a rather large rug was positioned in front of the office desk. When the other was on duty it was removed and put under the ward clock. My second experience of OCD! As soon as changeover of shift was complete the rug was repositioned as to their needs. I would lke to point out these 2 guys were extremely nice and very good at their job and apart from the rug issue they agreed on ward policy and care of the patients. Nothing was ever said between them or to others.

Main meal of the day was around midday to 1 o'clock. Evening meal at around 6pm where a varied selection of food was on offer. Sometimes this was soup. Cutlery was kept in a locked box in the store room and bear in mind there were up to 70 sets of cutlery and they had to be counted back in after a meal. A staff nurse who always reminds me of Mr McKay in the TV show

Porridge was explaining to me that in the evening not all cutlery was removed from the box, so if soup was on the menu for 20 patients you only needed to take out 20 spoons out then keep the key in your pocket and so you only had to count this amount back in, logic. He asked the other staff nurse who was a real comic how many spoons he had removed from the box, his reply was "about 3 hands full"

On another ward a patient had visitors from his family in Boston about once a month. They would bring all sorts of good things to eat e.g. pork pie, sausage rolls, cake and fresh eggs from the farm. When one particular charge nurse was on duty these items disappeared into his bag to take home. (Whether this was a survival thing or not as he had returned from a Japanese POW camp weighing about 4 stone, devastating in a man of 6 feet!) On one occasion the day before the items would disappear a staff nurse carefully injected the eggs with Paraldehyde, (a foul tasting sedative) and also removed the top layer of a sponge cake and added some faeces to the filling. We never found out how this went down when his wife prepared for her afternoon tea party!!! We do know it never happened again.

Qualified RMN in October 1963 and spent the next 2 years working as staff nurse on many of the wards I had previously worked as a student. All valuable experience.

Chapter Seven: On to Lincoln County Hospital to commence SRN training

In February 1966 I started my RGN training along with another student from St John's. We were a trial cohort to complete the course in 18 months as we were post graduates. We were qualified RMN and as such being sponsored and paid as trained nurses providing we returned to St John's for 2 years after completing RGN course.

This was the kind of nursing I always wanted to do. Lincoln County Hospital was a whole new experience, more friendly, and yet had a discipline code with clear guidelines on etiquette and procedure. On the first day we were in the classroom but had to go to the main dining room for lunch. It was very busy and only one table vacant that was set with tablecloth, napkins and fine cutlery, not knowing any different we retrieved our meal and proceed to sit at this table. We were aware of a sudden hush overtook the dining room suggesting something was wrong as all eyes were on us until someone very politely informed us this table was reserved for matron and her deputies. We very quickly found another table. The senior tutor was of small stature but had a fearsome personality. She was a very good teacher not only for the practical skills required but instilled the true values required to be a nurse. In spite of this she had a regular saying if you got things wrong "Nurse, if your patients get better, they do so, in spite of your treatment" She also had a keen sense of humour. She was the proud possessor of an Austin A30 car and even then she had seat belts fitted. One day she had just got in her car to go home and was putting on the seatbelt, on passing my mate remarked 'you'd think she was strapping herself in a Vulcan' Little did we know she had heard this remark but a few days later as my mate was going home on his motor bike and walking down the corridor in his leathers and crash helmet, he was met by Miss I who offered with a smile on her face "going flying Mr King?

"First ward experience on mens medical went quite well and I learned a lot and began to understand the protocols required. The turnover of patients was difficult at first to keep up with all that was happening with each one, especially when you had 2 days off and on returning you may not know anyone. Staff on this ward were extremely friendly, though very professional and made me welcome to a whole new experience of patient care. The ward sister was the ultimate professional and had an encyclopaedic knowledge of medical conditions and their nursing care and how they met the requirements of the total care of the individual. This is 1966 and smoking was allowed in almost any area of the hospital, the exceptions being the operating theatres (flammable gases) and wherever oxygen was being administered.

Sister was off for a long weekend and we were in the office having a drink, smoke and chat when someone set fire to the waste bin which left it a bit scorched and black. We hastily took it down to the works department for a repaint job. On her return sister was delighted with her flowery bin as opposed to the normal hospital grey and remarked it made the office much brighter!

My 2nd ward was mens surgical which, incidentally was the ward I eventually would be in charge of in 1970. I immediately became at one with surgery and knew this would be my ultimate goal to run this ward, I never thought it would happen, but it did. It had 28 beds made up of mainly general surgery but also had 6 ENT beds, 4 orthopaedic emergency (trauma), for immediate acute care and then were transferred to St Georges Hospital for ongoing care. Also in the mix were 2 maxillofacial beds as and when required? Enormous experience was obtained from these diverse specialities. It was always on standby for emergencies so each day was different to the next. There were days when we would be on emergency take for all of the specialities at the same time and it was not unusual to have up to 43 patients therefore having to put extra beds down the middle of the ward. The ward sister was skilled in all of these specialities and had teaching sessions whenever time allowed. This was one part of ward management I remembered for the future. At that time, one day a week we had to work a 'split 'shift, 7-1 break, then 5 until 9pm made it a long day. On the day of the world cup 1966 final Sister was on a split shift, so I was left in charge.

We weren't very busy and Sister told me to watch the final as long as the patients were ok. When she came back at 5pm the match had just gone to full time so she said "get off home" I lived on the other side of the city and as I was going home at breakneck speed I only saw 1 person, a policeman on Broadgate. I got home just as extra time started. The rest is history!

As part of preparation for a bowel investigation I was asked to give this patient a 3H enema (high, hot and helluva lot!) At this time there was no treatment room on any ward so all procedures had to be done at the patient's bed area with the curtains drawn. This ward was a 66 yards long Nightingale ward, the patients bed was half way down and the toilets were at the far end of the ward. So following the set procedure as part of preparation I took the commode chair to his bedside, explained the procedure and that when he felt the urge to empty his bowel to use the commode. This chap said "under no circumstance would he use the commode" I tried to explain that he would not make it to the toilet. I carried out the procedure and left him with curtains drawn around his bed and again reiterated for him to use the commode. After about 5 minutes he shot out from the curtains wearing nothing but his pyjama top, with his thumb up his arse running for the toilet with enema soap shooting like the wake of a ship spraying everything as he went. I am pleased the facilities did improve eventually and hopefully not another patient who thought he knew best.

Next came night duty, this is where you learned a lot and had to be very much focused. Bear in mind I was only a second year student and had to be in charge of the ward, with night sister on call if you got stuck. There were 2 night sisters on to cover the whole hospital 8 wards + Casualty. Shift times were 8pm until 0730. At 8pm you would receive report on all patients and at times was up to 40 different people, this could take up to half an hour. At 930 night sister would do her round of every patient, you were expected to know every patients name and diagnosis without referring to any notes. This was especially difficult when you had had a few days off as most of the patients were new to you. An enormous learning curve.

I will always remember the night I went on duty, 39 patients on the ward so we knew we would be busy. During the night unfortunately 3 had died but, at the end of shift we had 42 patients due to having 6 admissions. This was a busy night though everyone available came to help. All of the patients that had died had been using a certain brand of soap which, always became referred to by me as 'death soap' to the point of obsession. From that day I have never even touched the brand. My next door neighbour at the time had her father staying, who was terminally ill. Before retiring for the night I would always check to see if they were alright or needed anything. I went round as usual and they had been shopping and on the kitchen counter was a multipack of this soap. As I went home I said to myself "oh dear, this is the night" Sure enough I was woken up by the neighbour at about 3am asking me to go round as they thought dad had died, which he had. I still will not use any of this brand products.

Even in 1966 there were some nutters about. One of the night sisters had been threatened by a well know trouble maker after he was denied some Morphine for an imaginary disease during a visit to casualty. She rang me about 5am to say someone was roaming about in casualty and thought it was this chap and would I go to investigate whilst she looked after my ward. Casualty was not always busy during the night and invariably all the lights were turned off. I proceeded with caution and on entry into the unit it was about 3 steps to get to the light switch so I called 'ok Stanley no fucking about let's have you out of here' as soon as the lights were on it was obviously not who I thought it was but this chap wandering around seeking help as he had got some grit in his eye from an overtaking lorry whilst cycling to work. Needless to say he got star treatment after that!

Chapter eight: Transferred to St George's hospital to continue training

Transferred to St Georges Hospital, and first ward was Paediatrics and having never nursed children before was a frightening experience as this ward had new born and premature babies as well as toddlers up to 11 years old. First day was a mixed bag of experience, within the first 2 hours I had been pee'd on, vomited on and poo'd on, I soon learned how to avoid this. During this first day we admitted a premature baby who weighed 2.75 pounds. She was nursed in an incubator and had to feed via a tube which had to be passed into her stomach. Obviously I was taught how to carry out this procedure and 'J' became my very special baby. It was said anyone could know my off duty, if they looked at her feed and care chart as when I was on duty, no-one else was allowed to feed her! I was on this ward for 6 weeks and the day I left was the same day that J went home. I always remember she by then weighed 6 pounds and was able to take a full 6 ounce feed by mouth as normal. A by-line to this story is that some 12 years later after I had taken charge of Robey Ward in 1970, one Saturday afternoon a lady appeared on the ward and asked if she minded her having a look at the ward and wanted to show her daughter where she had once worked as a staff nurse. After talking to her for a few minutes and hearing of her experiences, I began to piece things together and said to her "your daughter then is called Chloe" the reply being she was but how did I know and I took great joy in telling her the story of her first 6 weeks of life and my involvement.

The sister on paediatrics was known to be very strict though for some reason I seemed to get on with her, One day when sister had gone for coffee break, the houseman came by and suggested a game of football on the lawn with the children. All good fun until the houseman kicked the ball over the 6 feet high fence and refused to go retrieve it so I went over the fence. Looking at my watch I realised sister would be back soon and in my haste got my trousers caught on a nail and had to gently get free. I hastily shot back, scrubbed up quickly and was sat down feeding a baby when sister popped her head round the door and said "that was very funny seeing you free your trousers arse from that fence". I learned a lot and sister allowed me to do all sorts of procedures under her supervision. I think I was also very lucky as no children died whilst I was on the ward.

Next came orthopaedic surgery.

This was a fun ward to work on as most of the patients were young, normally fit young men having many broken bones following road traffic accidents. As each one started to recover, their personality developed over the ensuing few weeks, some up to 15 -20 weeks. There was always good humoured banter between staff and patients,

One young man was having go at one the night male assistant nurses so, to get his own back the nurse went out the side door into a field where he found a hedgehog and took it back to the ward and when the cheeky little bugger was fast asleep he took out the hedgehog very gently laid in on his chest. A nice surprise when he woke up!!!

A young man of 16 years just starting to stoke up on his hormones had been in a motorbike accident and broke both shafts of femur and both wrists. Obviously the wrists healed quicker than the femurs and when the plaster casts came off he asked for them to be left as intact as possible. When a new nurse started on the ward, who he may have fancied, he would put the casts back on his wrists and then ask the nurse for a bottle to pee in. When she delivered said urinal he would look at his wrists and ask for some help. When the nurse went to collect the urinal he would take the casts of and politely thank her very much. Of cause the nurses only got caught once.

One young man who was on traction for a fractured femur and progressing well had asked for a bed pan for a poo. All I had to do was deliver the bedpan as by this time he was independent, whereupon he proceeded to lay toilet roll all along the bottom of the pan from front to back. His explanation was that lying in bed for 10 weeks and not getting any exercise he became quite constipated, only went about once a week and as there was always a lot, by this method you could do some and pull the paper forward thus avoiding it sticking on his arse.Sunday evening we always had a visit of the students from the ecclesiastical college when as many as possible beds were pushed together and a card school set in motion for real money. Good fun.

I spent Christmas on this ward and arrived on Christmas day for the late shift. The charge nurse promptly gave me the keys and said he would see me boxing day at 1 pm.

Another medical ward ensued with not much happening.

Matron of St Georges was known as being extremely strict. She was the proud owner of a black poodle dog, who went everywhere with her. One lunch time whilst having her meal in the dining room with all the senior managers, one of whom had an artificial limb the dog promptly decided to pee up the poor chap's limb. We who witnessed this event had to leave the dining room rather quickly so we could have a good laugh.

A student nurse was summoned to matron's office and as soon as she entered she was told 'good morning nurse, I hear you are pregnant, you leave at the end of the month,. The girl was in fact pregnant and left, had her baby and eventually returned to complete her training and eventually became a very well respected sister.

Chapter nine: Back to the County to complete training

Back to the County to continue with training.

Mens surgical. General surgery. Much the same as Robey but without the other specialities and of cause different surgeons. Again very good experience which; consolidated my ambition to progress my career in surgical nursing.

One day sister asked me if I would like to sit in whilst the registrar was informing some relatives that their father had a serious cancer of the bowel of which, at operation it was impossible to remove and altogether painted a rather grim picture as the prognosis was very poor and that he may die very soon. When he had answered their questions he said they could go in to see their father but do not be surprised as to his condition as he was a very poorly man. As we took them into the ward we were very surprised the chap was sitting up in bed with all sorts of tubes in situ and smoking a Woodbine with a smile on his face. You never ceased to be amazed by human beings.

Next came Casualty (Accident and Emergency)

As of now this department could be incredibly busy especially if a road traffic accident was expected. The unusual also happened quite frequently: One Sunday afternoon we had 5 patients who had all been bitten by donkeys, all different venues and different donkeys!

One of the most unusual was a chap arrived with a set of car keys on his penis which he couldn't get off. Apparently they were parked in a layby and his girlfriend suggested he put his keys on his todger and then have sex, all a bit bizarre but he went ahead anyway. The problem arose when he got an erection it would not go down because the key ring would not let the blood back from whence it came. He was in agony and all attempts to remove the key ring using the usual measures of soap and water, icepacks and we even broke 4 ring cutters because key rings are made of spring steel. It was by now beginning to look serious. The surgeon on call was called and as soon as he saw the problem he said "get me the duty engineer on call and tell them to get here as fast as he can and to bring some bolt cutters with him" The surgeon usually used to finer instruments proceeded to attach the bolt cutters to the key ring and held them in place whilst the engineer operated the cutters, the ring was quickly cut and removed and the crisis was over, This poor chap was very close to having his John Thomas amputated. The surgeon took the severed key ring and gave it to the girlfriend and told her 'not to so bloody daft in the future'.

Whilst we are talking about todgers; an A & E registrar told me of an incident, which; he swore was true whilst he was a junior Doctor in a Yorkshire city hospital. They had received 2 people both dead on arrival from a road traffic accident. As is normal practice they did post-mortems on both. Doing the male patient first it was noted his penis was missing and thought to have been a result of the accident. However, when the PM was performed on the female it was noted the guy's penis was in her mouth. The history of the accident was that they were parked in lay-by when a 10ton lorry ran into to the back of their vehicle. What a way to go!!!!

One afternoon a young man of about 25 yrs. arrived by ambulance with a suspected overdose of drugs. He was not very tall but was a fine muscularly young man who obviously worked out, I believe he was of Hungarian nationality. After been examined by the doctor it was decided he needed to have a stomach washout and then be admitted for ongoing care and psychiatric assessment. This procedure involves passing a tube down into the stomach, pouring warm water via a funnel down the tube, and then inverting the funnel into a receptacle to allow the stomach contents to empty. We had done this about 3 times when all of a sudden he shot up and jumped off the couch and along the way took a pair of scissors out of a nurses pocket and began threatening the staff. An alert was set in motion, first the doctor arrived, turned pale and hurriedly left the scene, then the plaster room technician arrived (who had already had 2 heart attacks) turned a funny shade of blue and had to sit down, then a porter arrived and suggested this was not within his pay grade. In the meantime we were trying to appease the guy and hopefully retrieve the scissors. The main thing I remember was my colleague another student nurse who was Irish and only about 5ft 2 inches stood hiding behind me saying in his Irish brogue "go on Sam, hit the fucker" Fortunately someone had thought to ring the police, who arrived at that moment and came in behind the chap, arrested, handcuffed him and took him into custody. It was all a bit scary at the time, but these incidents were frequent even then as of now, especially on Friday and Saturday nights.

One of the experiences whilst in A & E for some reason was you had to attend the sexual transmitted disease clinic (commonly known as the Clap Clinic) for 6 sessions. The Doctor in charge was a Glaswegian. New patients were very nervous, embarrassed and found it difficult to say what was wrong. The Doctor would look over his glasses and in the finest Glaswegian accent would suggest "so you think you've got the pox on your knob let's have a wee look laddie" and he would then proceed to use a pencil to lift up and examine the member. We used to get quite a lot of inmates from the prison who would arrive with a warder. On one occasion we had seen the prisoner and when he left for the waiting room and the next patient was called in, it just happened to be the warder who had escorted the prisoner. Fortunately, records were very confidential and all were referred to a special code number. For afternoon tea the doctor always brought fresh cream cakes, though I always pointed out I had an allergy to dairy foods and politely declined.

One winter's day there was about 6 inches of snow and still snowing. Casualty was absolutely packed and extremely busy. A fellow student who was 6ft 3in took it upon himself to walk out to the waiting room and got everyone's attention by announcing 'listen everybody, you can see how busy we are and the weather is awful as you can see and it is getting worse so, my advice would be, if you don't think you really need to be here then I would suggest you all get up and fuck off home' Within 10 minutes there was only 3 patients left in the waiting room.

One senior member of the staff would always insist the doctor should prescribe 75mgms of Pethidine for pain though most patients could take 100mgms without any problems. Pethidine is a controlled drug under the Dangerous Drugs Act because of its addictive properties and thereby had to be checked by 2 people, one of which must be an SRN. This person would always insist she would dispose of syringe etc., and the remaining 25mgms of the drug. It was sometime before I was told this 25mgms was always kept for herself for later!

At times when we were not busy and all the cleaning had been done, we could do what we liked as long as we could be reached. Not to waste any valuable time I always opted to go to the mortuary if there was a post mortem in progress. This was a first-hand opportunity to study anatomy which I found very useful. The mortuary technician was called Edward but was always referred to as Ted the dead!

Next came another general surgery ward as well as some ENT and ophthalmology.

A smaller ward but very busy and again valuable experience and reinforcing my ambition to eventually move my career to working in this area of nursing.

Next came my last placement as a student. Operating theatres.

The first thing you have to learn are the very strict protocols and correct procedures (this was before social distancing was even heard of!) Even where you are allowed to stand is important (depending on the job you are doing) Learning how to scrub up properly, and recognise who is scrubbed up and who isn't. You have to quickly get to grips with and remember all the components of a basic operating procedure set of instruments, about 60 pieces made up of scalpel handle, forceps of different types, sponge holders, retractors and many more, these were for every operation and then others were added for whatever particular procedure you were doing., so you could end up with up to 100 instruments for some operations. All swabs had to be counted and logged on the wall board and if further swabs were added these also had to be logged and confirmed by 2 people. This was incredibly important to know all these amounts as at the end of the operation when the abdominal wound was being closed, the scrub nurse and assistant had to confirm that 'swabs and instruments' correct, so as not to leave anything in the abdominal cavity.

One surgeon was scared of any electrical failure of the diathermy equipment and always stood on an anti-static mat, if any one got remotely close to this mat they were in no uncertain terms told 'to get of my fucking mat' I remember the first operation I assisted for was an above knee amputation of leg and as the operation was drawing to an end I was charged with holding the limb. I was not told how heavy this was going to be and when the whole leg was freed, it was heavier than I expected and promptly fell to the floor with this gangrenous leg on top of me. The amount of laughter that ensued told me I was not the first to suffer the indignity

Tension in an operating can be palpable and emotions could run high and difficult decisions having to be made. On one occasion a partial gastrectomy operation was taking place on an 81 year old lady who had a haemoglobin blood count of 18% due to having hematemesis and all medical treatment had not worked.

The operation was only about 15 minutes in when the anaesthetist said the lady was failing and the operation should end straight away. The surgeon insisted on carrying on and duly performed the fastest partial gastrectomy anyone had ever seen. The lady not only survived the operation but walked out of the hospital 10 days later.

Weekends were mostly spent cleaning the theatres, apart from if we had an emergency. It was a quiet time after the hustle and bustle of everyday life in an operating theatre. During operations there is a bowl set in a framework on wheels about 4 inches of the ground for disposal of swabs etc. during operations Another male student and I would sit in these frames and have a racing circuit around the theatres and corridors. One Saturday we both tried to go through a door at the same time and the other lad crashed into the wall, knocking off most of the tiles. We had to get a workman in to replace them.

As time progressed you began to feel confident to deal with most situations though we, as students never assisted consultants with special operations. This was left to the senior sisters which, never ceased to impress me as to their skill and professionalism throughout the whole team. Each surgeon had his own dedicated sister for difficult/special procedures. The amount of understanding, team work and mutual respect between surgeon and sister never ceased to amaze and impress me.

During this placement we had to do so many night duty shifts again, most of the time was spent cleaning and replacing stock for the following day. This also included cleaning the surgeon's wellies, if there was one who was not particularly nice you would always leave some water in them.

On one occasion we had a case of appendicitis that required appendectomy. This was good as we students would always have to scrub and the trained staff would pro for us. On this occasion I also had to monitor this patient during the recovery period. The porter was summoned to help transport her back to the ward but he had not arrived as Matron came down from her flat and she had had a few gin and tonics. She enquired what I was waiting for and suggested she would help take the patient back to the ward, politely informing me she was the most senior and would take the patients head end of the trolley and I would be the porter and do the pulling. The ward staff were amazed their patient had such exalted care.

On one occasion a young female arrived for removal of appendix and when preparing to start the operation it was noticed her pubic hair had been dyed green with a note in felt tip pen saying 'please keep of the grass. It was procedure that pubic hair had to be removed before operations of this type which was duly done along with a note saying 'sorry we had to mow the lawn '

It was general that you would avoid one surgeon as he was always very intense during operations and he would shout at you for the smallest thing. This man was an extremely good surgeon and nationally revered. On my last day with about an hour to go I was thinking I had avoided the ordeal when sister asked me to scrub for him doing a haemorrhoidectomy. Bugger. Everything went well until near the end he was completing the final dressing and had a special way of placing the small pressure packs around the anus. When the first pack was in situ I was told to hold it in place whist he placed the remaining 2. With the words "do not move "after a couple of minutes I think moved my leg for comfort. Stop moving the fucking pack I am told. I am only breathing was my reply. Well stop fucking breathing then. All good fun, but as was usual he thanked me for helping. 6 weeks in a thoroughly enjoyable area,

I was then and, am now in awe of the skills shown by surgeons. They are truly remarkable. So that's it, 18 months of the most enjoyable time is over and now have to go back to psychiatry to fulfil my contract. 6 weeks later I had the wonderful news that I had qualified SRN.

Chapter Ten: Back to t John's hospital

Back to St Johns to complete secondment agreement,
Very quiet after the hustle and bustle of the general
hospital. My first job as staff nurse was on a ward which,
had a lot of psychopaths which at that time was a new
area of psychiatry for the hospital. It was the only ward
that was locked at all times. Again a steep learning curve
to get to grips with an area of care that was new and
started whilst I was away doing my SRN training. The
charge nurse I worked with was relatively young but was
becoming an expert on this area of care. I learned a lot
from him and we developed a consistency of care when
either was days off. This was important and well
respected by the patients as most of them, as
psychopaths do tried to usurp the whole ward if they can.
The opposite shift had an older team but both teams
complimented each other and led to a good, effective
environment.

After having 18 months of harder physical work, extra
study, when I returned to a more sedentary and slower
pace environment I began to put on weight. I was
making an impact with diet and increasing exercise
albeit small. The charge nurse suggested I try one of his
wife's slimming pills as would he. We decided we would
do his on our weekend on, so we took one of the pills at
0700 on Saturday. Within an hour I had rang a student
who I had told off in the week and apologised to him. I
felt like I was walking on cotton wool clouds.

Throughout the day I had little to eat but drank plenty. My shift finished at 2100 so went home still buzzing, watched Match of the day and then the midnight movie. Went to bed at about 2am and was ready for work starting at 0600. When I got to work I got weighed and had lost half a stone! The other guy the same. So I asked what these magic pills were, the reply being 'Dexamphetamine sulphate' fucking hell I thought and was embarrassed that I did not question this the day before. Fortunately I did not get any come down or withdrawal effects. I stuck with the diet and exercise after that.

One day I worked an extra shift as a favour to my opposite number on the other shift. At coffee break the charge nurse said that he thought he had haemorrhoids and would the elderly staff nurse take a look? This staff nurse was in fact a retired, well respected charge nurse who was working odd shifts to supplement his pension. He was a very nice man, a perfect gentleman who happened to have diabetes type 1 and had developed retinopathy and subsequently had poor eye sight. He agreed to have a look and they proceeded into the office. A few minutes later the doctor came to do his ward round and asked where the boss was, we said he's in the office. The doc went to the office and opened it with his pass key and on pushing the door open he was confronted by the 18 stone charge nurse bent over his desk with his enormous trousers and pants round his ankles. On his knees was the staff nurse, prising apart the bum cheeks to inspect for piles. This was a close inspection due to his poor eyesight. The doctor took one look and remarked 'sorry lads' and promptly retreated. We were all in fits of laughter, you just could not write the script.

Chapter Eleven: Promoted to charge nurse

I was only back at St John's hospital about 3 months and was promoted to charge nurse. I was not given a permanent ward but was relief for anyone else absent for whatever reason and consequently moved around quite a lot. All good experience.

My first ward as a charge nurse was to shadow our old friend BE who, by this time had his own ward. On my first day I was asked to give the drug cupboard a good clean out as I had just completed my SRN! (Not sure why that made me a good cupboard cleaner) During this procedure I came across a box which; contained 48 x 2mls ampoules of LSD. The other 2 had been used for abreaction therapy some 2 years before. At this time LSD was not controlled by the Dangerous Drugs Act, so no records were kept. On the black market these were worth an awful amount of money. I did return them to the pharmacy.

A charge nurse that had the respect of everyone including me. He was a gentle giant whose real name was Bill but because of his gingery coloured hair he was always known as Nutty. He had the most wonderful sense of humour and once told me that in the life of everyman there were 5000 shags and 200 wanks and he had 2 of each left! He also held the theory that in the first 2 years of marriage or other relationship, if you put a pea in a jar for every time you had sex and after 2 years you would take out 1 pea for every time, that you would never get the jar empty! He told me a friend of his, when he was younger, who was a charge nurse on night duty had a condom that he used over and over and that at one point he had repaired it with a bike inner tube puncture repair kit!!!!

Chapter Twelve: Working 9 to 5 in Rehabilitation Centre

I only did the relief duties for a short while when a vacancy came up for deputy in the rehabilitation unit. This was 8 to 5 Monday to Friday and every weekend off. There were 2 units on site one of which was called the 'piggeries' as it was based in the part of the hospital that previously had kept its own farm animals. There was also a very well kept garden which produced a variety of vegetables and fruit, apples, pears, raspberries, strawberries and many more.

We had contracts with a box company, all sizes of boxes came flat packed and had to be assembled, although the task was somewhat mundane it facilitated a lot of conversations as to the close proximity of working. It was somewhat competitive as deadlines had to be met. The 2 ladies who ran the day to day unit, to make it more interesting would set up a competition atmosphere which, was always enjoyed and it encouraged camaraderie. The patients really enjoyed being a part of this team.

In one section of this unit was an area where stacking nets were made for the local farmers, again the guys enjoyed this. One guy in particular, an Irishman who was always called Paddy except by 2 people, an Irish charge nurse and the other was me and we called him by his first name 'Patrick'. He was a very intelligent chap who suffered with well-controlled paranoid schizophrenia. I had first met him on the first ward after doing my SRN training and he actually taught me how to play the card game 'Solo' I always remember he used to call me 'a sheep brained bugger' if I got it wrong. We did in fact get on very well. An add on to this is I had gone back to Lincoln County and after about a year we needed some cardboard to make decorations for the ward so, I went back to the unit to pick up any spare boxes. I had taken my daughters who were age 4 and 7 years old. On my way into the unit I passed by the net making room, I called in "good morning Patrick" he had his back to me and replied without seeing me "morning Sam" when he turned round and saw the girls he came over and rolled down his shirt sleeve where he kept his money and gave them £5 each.

■■■

n the other purpose built unit there was a fully fitted kitchen and a wood work shop each with its own instructors. In the main room a variety of activities were carried out and I remember we had a contract with a garden magazine who were giving away free rose bushes. These were supplied by a company in Spalding. We had to sort out all the pre-printed address labels in to the respective post codes and then prepare and pack the roses with the correct label to be collected by Royal Mail. I think I had the best rose garden in our road!!!

As we had dealings with various companies throughout Lincolnshire it meant one of us (4 in all) were out travelling quite a lot which; was most enjoyable as most companies would provide lunch or take you out to have a meal on expenses. As part of the rehabilitation programme we were challenged to find recovering patients a job. We built up relationships with companies all over Lincolnshire and in particular Lincoln City itself. We owed a debt of gratitude to all of them who took part and indeed some degree of risk in taking it on board, what was to them an unknown entity. We in turn were very careful with the placing of patients, primarily what would be best for the patient but also what would be the benefit to the company. Review and conversation was the key to any success. In the case of some patients we had to be careful when asked to find someone job as you always felt no matter who you asked, you would know it could be doomed to fail and the chances were that the company would not agree to any further requests for placements.

By far the most helpful employers were British Steel in Scunthorpe because they had a very good HR team and backup systems already in place. We were able to get jobs for the patients in a number of departments with a huge amount of success. This was the senior member of the team's pet project. Every Thursday he would make the trip to review the progress of all participants, sometimes I would go with him as when he was off I had to go on my own. This was usually a delightful day primarily, to see the success of the project but, we were always very well received and usually had lunch in the executive dining room. This of cause was when British

Steel was a successful company. It was fascinating to see how steel was made, and also frightening at how dangerous it could be. Very few accidents occurred but when they did they were usually serious. The on-site medical facilities were excellent and run by one of my friends from my student days. The site had its own priest who was vicar of one of the villages between Lincoln and Scunthorpe. An extremely likable, good humoured man who could tell the filthiest of jokes I had ever heard. One Thursday on our visit he said he would take us out for lunch to a pub in town. We duly proceeded to this back street pub which did not serve food. The vicar told us this was only a stop off on the way to a restaurant but he wanted to show us something and asked had we noted anything unusual with the female drinkers sitting opposite. Well not really so he said' look at the soles of their shoes' which had the price of a good time written on them thus, allowing one to choose and at what price you could afford! I don't know whether this was unique or if it happened in other industrial or fishing towns?

All in all this was a good job with very little pressure. Plenty of autonomy, not at all boring, a lot of trips all over Lincolnshire and every weekend off. My colleagues thought I was potty still wanting to go back to general nursing with the hard work and pressure that went with it.

Chapter thirteen: Interview for dream Job!

In the summer of 1970 I had been on holiday for 2 weeks and on my return a friend rang me to say that the ward I always wanted had been advertised but I had missed the closing date. Bugger!!So don't give up Sam. I really can't lose anything, so I rang matron at Lincoln County and asked if the job had been taken and if not, could I apply? Her reply being 'That she had been interviewing that morning and no it has not been taken and by all means do apply' She went on to say she remembered me as a student and that she was on holiday for 2 weeks so I had time to get my application in. Phew!

About 3 weeks later I had an interview. The letter sent said Matron and Consultant surgeon would be the interviewers. The interview seemed to be going well until an enormous wasp came in through the open window. The usual 'panic' ensued, so I stood up and suggested I open the window a bit wider and the wasp, as if by magic exited. After the interview was over I went down to the ward to see the sister and staff who I knew quite well.

A few minutes later Matron popped her head round the corner and said" a letter would be in the post later, dear and I am sure we will be seeing you soon" Happiest man on the planet! I eventually began to realise the importance of this role, the hard work involved this career change would bring. I must admit I was beginning to feel anxious even though this was what I wanted to do way back in my early career.

Chapter Fourteen: Started as Charge Nurse (Surgery) LCH

First 2 days on induction and administrative essentials. Visits to every department and general introduction to the overall running of the hospital. Any spare time spent getting to know my team. I still could not believe it and was so excited. This skinny kid from Amber Hill with the safety pin to hold up his trousers was here doing the job I wanted. It was also quite daunting having only done 2 years RGN training and here I was being responsible for the running of a surgical ward. Although I had kept up to date as much as possible during the preceeding3 years. Fortunately, the first week of being 'in charge' the ward was not too busy. My first job was to meet with the trained members of the team who had an enormous amount of experience and I would need to rely on them to help me through the first few weeks. The last time I had worked with most of them, I was a student and they were the seniors, now I was in charge with a great act to follow from the previous sister, who had been promoted to assistant matron responsible for the surgical unit. The first few weeks were hard work for me, getting to grips with the procedures, specialist skills and knowledge requirements of 6 different surgeons over 4 specialities. I will always be grateful for the help I received from all the ward team and the understanding of the consultants. At this time the hospital was run by senior consultant surgeon and consultant physician, a hospital; secretary and not least by a matron. They were extremely well respected and led the whole staff with loyalty, respect, humility, support and understanding. I think one of the main reasons was that by today's standards it was a small unit and the senior staff, especially matron, knew everyone, from the most senior to the most junior and they were always treated as an equal part of the family with equal respect.

I remember I was asked to join the student nurse support and welfare group that met about twice a year to advise on how best the students were supported and basically looked after, especially if they lived in the nurse's home. At this meeting the person in charge of ordering equipment reported that nurses' capes should cease to be supplied as they were too expensive. This was immediately rebuffed by the consultant surgeon with the words" don't be silly man, how would you like to walk over from the nurses home for a shift starting at 7 o'clock in the morning in the ice, snow, wind or rain, keep ordering them" no further discussion ensued and capes continued to be provided. At that time there was special sister who was in charge of the nurse's home who was responsible for the welfare of all residents particularly the student nurses. She also co-ordinated the hospital physician (basically the hospital GP) it was also her duty to check that all nurses were dressed appropriately as they went on duty. If they did not have a vest on 'on cold mornings 'they were told to go and put one on!!

Etiquette was also strictly kept and certainly made discipline easy to follow, if you met a senior member of staff, particularly matron, on the corridor you were never allowed to speak unless she spoke first. Every Tuesday matron did her ward rounds, on entering the ward she would always address me by surname and ask if it was convenient to meet the patients, if I was busy she would be escorted by any other member of staff who, hopefully knew all the patients names and diagnosis. On completion of the round she would always come to me to say Mr Whoever would like to see me for whatever reason. This obviously told me 1. That she was senior and 2. That she never missed anything. Within half an hour of the visit she would ring the ward and ask me to go to her office. On entry to the office matron would be sat with her feet on the desk smoking a cigarette, offer me one and a cup of coffee. Sit down Sam, then we would chat about anything while taking coffee.

One Saturday afternoon we received a call from casualty (now A&E) to say could we expect a Mr Bear who had been involved in an RTA. Mr E Bear was duly brought round on a stretcher complete with a set of notes. He was rather a nice little Teddy Bear who had been found on the road side. He was made comfortable in bed and formally admitted and notes made with his own folder, place in the notes trolley. Sounds a bit daft really and was instigated by a 3rd year student who had recently been part of our team and on qualifying became a staff nurse and returned to work on Robey ward. The bear quickly became recognised as the ward mascot and treated with respect. One of the domestic team knotted him some clothes and a scarf. When his bed was needed for a human patient he was placed on top of the emergency call control panel. One day I was talking to an assistant matron with our backs to the panel, we both turned at the same time and someone had put a glyceine suppository poking out of his trousers. Miss??? Made a hasty retreat with a 'really that's disgusting' It was so unexpected from my point of view that I thought it was hilarious. It was well known throughout the hospital that he was our mascot and had been for a long time. For this reason he was kidnapped by the orthopaedic ward sister and a ransom had to be paid to get him back. I distinctly remember the demands were rather threatening and I knew where they were coming from. No figure was mentioned but we set out to raise as much as we could (all the cash raised was to go to pay the ransom and would be given to the BBC's children in need appeal) every one donated money from the consultants, doctors and all other members of the MDT and included the domestic team and some patients and their relatives also contributed. We eventually raised £200 to be donated and Mr Bear was returned unharmed.

Chapter Fifteen: Getting to know the role.

Over time you would build a rapport with the consultants, each having differing personalities, past histories and of cause their specialities. It was important to get to know these individual traits to enable a smooth running of the ward and most importantly ensure the correct care was delivered o the patient. Junior Doctors and Registrars would rotate about every 6 months and it was expected the nursing team would be instrumental in ensuring the consultant's standards and procedures were followed. This sometimes caused difficult situations especially with registrars as they were usually qualified surgeons in their own right but gaining post graduate experience. I remember one incident at a weekend where a patient who had had a prostatectomy the previous Thursday was still bleeding more than usual, his post op blood count was also low. I asked the registrar if he would write the patient up for 2 units of blood which he refused to do as he felt it unnecessary. I was always reluctant to ring a consultant at the weekend but felt on this occasion it was justified to explain that I was concerned. Ten minutes later the registrar returned and said on reflection I think we will transfuse this chap. These incidents were rare but had to be acted on if in doubt.

Another occasion I rang my consultant at home as during a Monday morning, after one of my staff had come to the ward early (she was due on shift at 1pm) she was very upset and told me she had found a suspicious swelling in her breast. I explained to the consultant the problem and he said "ask her not to have anything to eat or drink, he would come in early for his operating list at 1345, examine her and if necessary he would do a biopsy first on his list "Fortunately, it was nothing to worry about, though very reassuring that we all looked after each other. This consultant was always a perfect gentleman who treated everyone with respect. As far as I remember a bad word was never said about him. He was always extremely well respected by his colleagues. I remember him doing an emergency bowel operation at a week-end. Apparently this was an extremely difficult procedure. Post op when the anaesthetist came to check on the patient she told me it was the finest piece of surgery she had witnessed in all of her 30 years' experience.

The ultimate was when he came to me and asked if I would give him an injection of Penicillin prior to him having some dental work done that afternoon. It was a privilege to work with GTC. About 3 years after he had retired, I was playing golf at the club he was a member. I was most surprised when he had walked over 3 fairways to say hello.

This was the normal standard of care that all members of received. If any member of staff needed surgery it was always procedure that 1.the consultant would do he operation themselves, 2. Would have consultant anaesthetist. 3. The person in charge of the ward team would personally take the patient to theatre and 4 hand them over to a theatre sister. 5. Fetched from recovery by person in charge of the ward. This was the same standard procedure for all members of staff whatever their job role.

Occasionally, we would admit emergencies when 'on take' that had been previously treated by one of the other surgeons who had beds on another ward. Protocol was they would take them to their own ward after review. One particular surgeon would arrive to review his patient and invariably he would be smoking a cigarette. He would take a half-crown out of his pocket, place it on the corner of the ward desk on which he would put his ciggie, go and examine his patient and retrieve his smoke, pocket the half-crown before giving any instructions and subsequently leaving the ward. One day he forgot the half-crown which I still have to this day.

When he was 'on take' this surgeon along with his own friendly anaesthetist would stay in the surgeons' room until midnight after been served cocoa at 1145. The doctors on call would then have to give a report on every patient who was causing concern so that he could sort them out before going home.

Now when out walking I occasionally walk through the cemetery and go past his very simple head stone and think about his impact on care and the memorable episodes, some funny, some sad but always a pleasure to remember.

One day I was not very busy and had the time to go and watch an operation on an aortic aneurism, this was as big as it got. I was amazed at the skills involved not only from a surgery point of view but also, the skill of the anaesthetist working together. I was even more impressed when half way through the procedure, the surgeon and anaesthetist re-enacted a scene from Black Adder with the whole of people present in fits of laughter. The patient did go home 10 days later.

Over the years I have worked with some extraordinary surgeons of whom, I have the greatest respect for their skill, stamina, and dedication. I was very fortunate that over this time when surgeons' retired and new consultants came, in that I was always learning how to care for a continuing range of new conditions and their needs.

Talking of retirements, one of the consultants relayed the story of going to a retirement event for one of his peers who was an ophthalmic surgeon. As part of the proceedings his team had commissioned a painting depicting an eye and in the pupil area was a very good portrait of the retiring surgeon. In his acceptance speech he related how pleased he was with the extraordinary unique gift but he was also delighted that he had not been a gynaecologist!!

One day I was taking a patient to theatre as he was first on the list at 2pm, on the way up in the lift the patient said that he didn't feel very well. I explained that it was probably the premedication he had been given and that we were almost in the theatre. The anaesthetist introduced himself and explained what he was going to do. The patient re-iterated that he didn't feel well and promptly had a cardiac arrest. Everything possible was done to save him but all to no avail. The surgeon who kept popping his head around the door remarked to the anaesthetist." I think we will take an early tea Charles" The mandatory post-mortem showed he had an inoperable cancer of the stomach, so in many ways no matter how sad this was he was spared some pain and suffering.

The story goes this particular anaesthetist, who was an absolute gentleman was on his way back from Australia by plane when a stewardess came to him and "excuse me sir there is a man at the back of the plane who is on the point of collapse and as we thought you are a doctor that you may be able to help. He looked up from his book and announced "sorry PHD history"

As was usual practice anaesthetists would visit their patients the evening before the surgery. One such evening 5 anaesthetists visited all at the same time. My remark was 'what is the collective term for a group of anaesthetists, as quick as a flash one replied 'just a whiff '

I was asked by the consultant if I would assist him to perform a laryngectomy as he did not have a houseman who would do this normally. This is an operation where the larynx is removed along with the vocal cords because of cancer, the patient would be left with a permanent tracheostomy and would need to breathe through a stoma which opened at the front of the neck and would need to learn how to speak again basically by regurgitating air from the oesophagus and forming words using his mouth and tongue, takes a lot of time, patience and determination on their behalf. Although I said I was asked to assist in reality, all I did was hold a retractor and assist in suturing the wound on completion. This was a fascinating operation to watch, the surgery so delicate which took 4 hours to complete. These were the only sutures ever I helped to put in and eventually remove. Removal of sutures for this operation was a specialist procedure as you had to observe for any leaks which, denoted the wound had not healed inside and meant the patient could not eat or drink until the healing had taken place. Feeding was via a naso-gastric tube and followed a comprehensive nutritional plan. Occasionally if they liked a drink we would pour some whisky or brandy down the tube whilst allowing them to sniff the glass thus getting the effect!! The first 24 hours these patients had to be 'specialled' as at this time no ICU existed! This meant a trained nurse had to be with them 24/7 and each team member who had this role always felt their 'special' was the best. The patient whose operation I had seen was specialled by my senior staff nurse who was his dedicated nurse until he went home. She obviously worked very hard to help him fully recover. She was absolutely delighted that on the morning he was going home that he met her half way down the ward and said in his oesophageal voice "good morning Sue" He went on to develop an extremely good voice and was able to use the telephone amongst other things. I used to deliver a training session to student nurses on this operation and this patient was always willing to participate as part of the talk to show what could be achieved in this situation. He showed me a letter he had received from a famous actor who had had a laryngectomy wishing him well. Every year I would get a Christmas card from him and after his death some 25 years later, this was carried on by his wife for a number of years.

Chapter Sixteen; Some Consultant funny stories!

We had a young man of 14 years who was recovering from a road traffic accident sustaining a severe concussion and had been unconscious for about 3 weeks. Every week on the ward round the consultant would take one look and dictate to his secretary for the notes 'ISQ' or no real change. On this occasion I interjected with 'he seems to be making progress, interacting and beginning to walk with aid' the consultant said to him "you seem to be getting better James" to which James replied " I have to get out of bed and start walking or else Sam will kick my arse"

I don't suppose we could get away with this in today's environment. We had a 90 years old gentleman who had had a fall and suffered some concussion, of which he made a very good recovery. The consultant said he could go home. He was the grandfather of a member of staff who wanted to redecorate his bungalow as a surprise when he went home and could he have a few more days to finish the work, to which I agreed. On the next ward round we came to this gentleman's bed, the registrar turned to me in horror as he would probably get a roasting for keeping this gentleman in. He was relieved when I informed him that I had hidden him the day room until after the ward round.

One consultant enjoyed teaching and commanded an audience of all the team. These talks covered many aspects of human biology and anatomy and were incredibly interesting. Over the years I had attended most of these and when it came to the questions part of the lecture I had remembered all the answers to which I could get called 'swot 'or most likely 'clever shit'by the doctors especially if they did not know the answers.

On one ward round this consultant was examining a patient and noticed he had a misshaped finger (nothing to do with what he was in for) he then proceeded to give a talk on congenital abnormalities of digits. At the end he turned to the patient who's hand he had been holding during the talk and said to him "has anyone else in your family got a misshaped finger" to which came the reply "no and I didn't until I broke it 10 years ago" We quickly moved on!!

Another occasion we had a post op patient who we suspected had had a stroke during the night and we requested the physician team to check him out. During the time he was being examined by the medial team this consultant arrived before his operating list that afternoon. All the medical team made room for the consultant who took the history and proceeded to examine the patient. As part of this every doctor have their own way of looking for any paralysis particularly the face, some would ask them to close their eyes tight, others may ask them to smile. On this occasion the consultant asked the patient to show him his teeth, the patient promptly leaned over to his bedside table and picked up the pot with his false teeth in and presented them for inspection. In spite of all these little funny episodes, this consultant was a perfect gentleman and an extremely talented surgeon. Very skilled and well respected, I admired and enjoyed working with him a lot. A great learning experience.

Chapter Seventeen: Some funny and sweet nurse stories

There are also some funny nurse stories, all of them as far as I know are true.

Very new students (the ones who were green and thought to be able to take a joke) were very often embarrassed by the trained staff when asked to go to another ward for a long stand. They would present to the other ward who also knew this joke and after ignoring them for 5 minutes would say "thank you nurse I think you have been standing long enough" surprising how many fell for this. Another one was asking them to go to another ward and ask if they could borrow some Fallopian tubes. A distinct advantage to know your anatomy.

A ward sister asked a student if she would give a patient 2 Aminophylline suppositories to help his breathing as he was having some bronchospasm. After checking out the prescription the nurse proceeded to the patient, she then returned to sister and said she had completed the task and disposed of the waste. Something rang a bell in sisters' mind so she went to check any improvement the patient may be having only to find him sat up in bed with a suppository poking out of each nostril. I know, they may as well have been shoved up his arse!

■■ ■

On a care of the elderly ward a junior nurse was asked if she would go round the ward and carry out catheter toilet to help prevent infection. This usually was simply to clean the catheter where it goes into the urethra, check it was comfortable and working ok. About 10 minutes later she appeared at sister's office with about 10 catheters in her hand and said "I have cleaned them all, sister but who is going to put them back in? "This ward had a policy of ensuring the patients dentures were removed at bed time, unless of course they objected. He nurse was instructed to check all the patients, remove and clean dentures. For some reason she actually collected all the dentures in one bowl and cleaned them, only to realise she did not know who's were who's teeth!

Another true but rather sweet story. It goes that a patient had died and sister asked the student nurse to make sure he looked presentable and the room tidy as his wife was coming to see him. Halve an hour passed and nurse reported she had completed the job and thought the patient's wife would be pleased to see him for the last time. Again sister intuition 'what has she done' and went to the room and the patient was sat up in bed supported by pillows, hair brushed, false teeth in, spectacles on, with his knees drawn and he was holding a newspaper. When asked her rationale for this the nurse said "this gentleman was always at his happiest when reading the Telegraph sports page and I thought his wife would like to remember him doing something he enjoyed"

∎∎

In 1971 there was the first of a few Bardney pop festivals with an attendance of some 50,000 to see the likes of Beach Boys, Rod Stewart, Roxy Music, Slade, Status Quo and Don McLean perform in a muddy field. All routine operations were postponed as we thought we may be getting a lot cases, the hospital was virtually empty. In fact we only had 1 patient, an American admitted with a broken leg having fallen off his motorcycle.

At the time of the festival in the days leading up to it, I had on my ward a very officious, mature 2nd year student nurse who always said we could not teach her anything, that was until I asked her to remove some sutures, she shamefacedly had to admit she didn't know how. A couple of days before the festival a post graduate psychiatric student, who I knew very well was putting the drug order away in the medicine cupboard situated in the clinical area where said nurse was washing her hands before going off duty. I asked, giving him a wink if we had ordered enough of the little blue and green pills for the following week. He looked at me and winked acknowledgement and replied 'sure and the little red ones that go down well' Said nurse proceeded to go off duty. I said to Mick 10 minutes and he said probably 5 and at 5 minutes the phone rang, matron. Can you come down to my office where the chief pharmacist was waiting and said we had been reported as going to sell drugs at the pop festival. Fortunately matron was well aware of the nurses' reputation and saw the funny side of this.

Chapter Eighteen: Patients remembered!

Over the years I met and got to know many people and remember most of them, though some now a distant memory. There are of cause a number of people and situations you never forget. One chap in particular had been admitted following an industrial injury sustaining a back injury. He was only in my ward about 4 days and then transferred to St Georges orthopaedic ward for further investigation eventually being discharged and having a planned course of physiotherapy. At that time the physiotherapy department was just up the corridor from my ward. When he attended for his treatment he would always call to see us on the ward and have a cup of tea. He always walked with 2 sticks and over the weeks never seemed to be improving. After some time he came in one day, no sticks, walking fine and very happy. I remarked how well he was and what had brought along this remarkable improvement. The reply being 'he had received his compensation settlement from his employers which was very considerable at the time for his industrial injury and he had used some of it to visit Lourdes, he added that when he came out of the shrine, he could walk properly again and had no pain. Truly a miracle!!

■■■ ■■ ■

One guy who had had an illustrious career as a prison officer was about 6ft 2in and looked like he would be scared of no-one and the toughest criminal would think twice about tackling him. I was astounded by the stories of procedures and notoriety that he relayed, none of which I cannot repeat in this forum. He had quite a serious kidney problem and was absolutely scared of anaesthesia and surgery in general. I don't know why but he always thought I was his lucky talisman. When he was due to come in for anything to be done he would always ask if I was on duty on the day of his surgery and the timing of his operation was always timed that I would be free to take him to theatre and stay until he had the anaesthetic and I had to wait in recovery for when he came out of surgery and became awake. On one occasion I was on holiday and he refused to be admitted until I came back. He had a lovely wife who would come in to see us long after the poor chap had died.

Another special man from an outlying village who was a builder and well respected throughout the village. The story goes that on his workmen's pay day the village elders would arrive at the yard gates and would be given a gift of whatever their pleasure, packet of ciggies, bottles of beer or even cash if they had no other vices! On the day of admission as an emergency his wife was unpacking his bag and proceeded to put 20 packets of Players Navy Cut cigarettes in his bed side locker, I suggested she might wish to take some of them home as

I was sure he would not be well enough to smoke that many. It turned out he had a serious abdominal problem that required 3 major operations to sort out. He never did smoke another cigarette but in between the operations when he was well enough he had a pipe which had a ball of cotton wool in that he would pretend to be creating a small cloud. He had a lot of ups and downs over a period of weeks and we really got to know the family well, including the local Baptist minister who was a regular visitor and one of the nicest, down to earth people I have ever met. Inevitably due to his condition he contracted a serious infection and had to be barrier nursed. For about a week he was extremely toxic and delirious, but he made a good recovery and eventually went home. He popped in to see us when attending outpatients and over cup of tea he relayed the story of when he was coming out of the delirium he remembers me going into his room to say good morning and said that at the time he was on top of a roof retold the story of when he was delirious he thought he was on a shed roof with no means of getting down and asked me to help, apparently I replied 'don't be so fucking daft you are in hospital'. This gentleman and his family were very special indeed and had the respect and admiration of the whole team.

Over the years we had a variety of what would be called in today speak 'celebrities' admitted or visiting, I remember a News reporter/reader from the BBC with concussion, the brother of a famous comedian and many more when they were performing at the Theatre Royal, very often we would get complimentary tickets to the shows. The most memorable of all who came to visit the children's ward is my all-time favourite footballer Bobby Charlton, what a nice chap and an honour to meet him.

Talking of football, we often had Lincoln City players admitted especially after a good kicking local game against Scunthorpe or Grimsby. On one of these occasions I had the pleasure to meet Graham Taylor, the then manager of Lincoln City he was obviously at that time on the way up but never the less enjoyable to meet such a real nice guy. On this occasion it was City's captain who had sustained a facial injury playing against Scunthorpe, He just happened to live not far from me and would come by my house when out running. It was a great surprise when 2 complimentary tickets for the very last game between England and Scotland at Wembley were put through my letter box.

We had in a patient who happened to be captain of a local golf club. I also played to a reasonable handicap, and we would talk a lot about the game in general terms when I had the time to spare. Just before he was due to go home he asked me if I would like a free trip to the USA. One of the perks of being club captain was this free trip to a club manufacturer's headquarters in, I think was Houston, Texas. Of course I would be silly to turn this down. The date for the trip was agreed for 4 months hence. About 2 months before we were due to go, his wife rang me to say her husband had had a heart attack and hadn't survived. A very sad day all-round.

One of the first patients I had was a school teacher and on my round to meet all the patients. He was reading a comic, Dandy or Beano or some such. I thought immediately he was an affable sort of chap and I jokingly remarked what was an intelligent man like him doing reading comics. This was the start of a friendship which has lasted for 50 years.

Chapter Nineteen: Some not so nice patients, sad really.

Not all patients were particularly likeable and some obnoxious however, we tried to meet their needs no matter how difficult it may have been. Of note one chap who had relatively small operation was due to go home. A nurse came to me and asked why this man should have poo'd in his bed, to which I had no immediate answer, so went to check him out. On asking him what was the problem he pointed to the daily paper where the headline was that 'nurses to get a good pay rise' and he suggested in no uncertain terms "you have a pay rise and are paid to clean up my shit so get on with it". He was escorted of the ward rather quickly.

Another chap was going home and I went to him with his medication and GP letter and popped my head around the curtains to see him trying to close his suitcase, I asked if I could give him a hand as there was obviously something preventing the lid from closing. On closer inspection it was plain to see it was a hospital sheet that was causing the problem and when the lid was open, inside the case were 4 sheets and 2 pillowcases. I removed them with the suggestion they would not fit a double bed and not really stylish to have 'property of Lincoln County Hospital' stamped through the centre. I left it at that and eventually he went on his way with a half empty case.

We had £100 given to us by a grateful patient to buy something for the benefit of the patients. As the hospital radio was only working at intervals, we decided to buy a radio/cassette player and set of headphones, all the staff were given a cassette to record their favourite music, thus ensuring a rich selection to choose from. This worked very well until about 2 weeks later it disappeared having been stolen by a patient, we knew who it was, but could not prove it.

During the late 70's and 80's there was a mass exodus from London to the north but they wanted to stay within commuter distance to London, a lot settled in the Grantham area because of good rail and road links. Grantham only has a small hospital and very often had to transfer some patients to Lincoln County. It always seemed some of these patients had a bit of a superior complex, in that they came from London and were better than us in the North. Most, I must add were very nice. On one occasion we had in a right 'gob shite' who had one of his legs amputated for peripheral-vascular disease, He was really an obnoxious fellow who would pick up on any slight difference in people and very loudly express it all, for example: if someone had no hair, he would shout "here he comes old bleb head" or some that could not walk very well he would shout "bloody hell he's pissed again" or if some had a urethral catheter on drainage he would proclaim "here he comes with a pipe up his knob because he can't piss properly".

I cannot repeat his observations of the black/Asian medical team. I did talk to his family to ask if they could help but they replied that he had always been like this but, acknowledged how embarrassing it was for the family as well. On one occasion a nurse was walking towards his bed when he announced in his loud voice" here she comes the nurse with the chubby legs" She stopped by his bed and replied in an equally loud voice "but at least they both reach the ground" A round of applause ensued from all the other patients. He was very quiet after his and fortunately transferred back to Grantham Hospital 2 days later.

A very grieved son of one of the patients who had been told of his fathers' inoperable cancer by the consultant, became most irate and accused the surgeon of incompetence telling lies, this was not an unusual reaction however this chap took it one step further by going to Gainsborough hospital and on identifying the surgeons' brand new car in the car park and proceeded to pour anti-freeze and brake fluid solution all over it doing many pounds worth of damage.

Chapter Twenty: Catheter experiences!

When 'on take' we would get a few admissions of patients with acute retention of urine, usually caused by enlarged prostate gland affecting most men over about 50 yrs. Not so much public information and campaigning was done at that time and obviously now people are living longer and the prevalence of enlarged prostate has subsequently increased, likewise publicity has also increased. Today surgery is available for this but usually as a last resort. Modern medicine has moved on with good results thankfully. In the 70s, 80s and 90s when I was mostly involved, surgery was the main option providing the patient was fit as they usually were because of their age.

Saturday afternoon was quite common to have these patients admitted as they had probably sunk a few pints of beer before going to see Lincoln City play, they would stand on the terraces and at half time would grab a pie and a pint of tea, then not wanting to miss the start of the second half they would delay going for a pee. I remember one such chap came in who was in absolute agony and could not even lie on the bed. The doctor did a quick examination of abdomen and agreed the full bladder and asked if I would do the catheterisation. This was the first and only time I had to perform catheterisation of a patient whilst he was stood up. He was so glad to be pain free and able to now lie down and sleep off his beer.

I was fortunate and proud to work with 2 brilliant urological surgeons who achieved excellent results. One of the principal side effects of prostatectomy is the likelihood of impotency but as far as I am aware the incidence of this was rare, mainly due to the skill of the surgeon. The patients prior to giving consent for the operation had to be informed of this side effect, but because we had confidence in the surgeon we were able to be very optimistic about the outcome. I was stopped on the high street by a patient who had had this operation a few weeks before. After some vigorous hand shaking and hugs from his wife who happened to be about 15 yrs. younger than him and a very attractive Swedish woman with a twinkle in her eye, they both were pleased to inform me sex had never been so good!!

The oldest gentleman we nursed after a prostatectomy was 91 but very fit. He was not very tall, very proud of his 60 years old wife who, adored him. He was a country boy who had a very simplistic outlook on life. One day he was talking about his family (he was born in 1880) he said ' he had a brother who died during the Spanish flu epidemic just after it came out, adding appendicitis came out at the same time and you used to die from that as well!) What a wonderful turn of phrase. On the third day post op he accidentally stood on his drainage bag and pulled his catheter out (normally left in for at least 7 days) rather than repass a catheter which could have some dangers, we decided to see how things went. In fact they went very well and he went home on the 7th day post op. He actually went back to work about 2 weeks later.

After prostatectomy we had to remain positive that control and continence would return within a couple of weeks or so and then they would be able to pee like a wild stallion. I was doing the weekly shop in a supermarket and a voice came over from the next aisle "hiya Sam, you were right mate, I could piss on you from here"

Chapter Twenty One: Everyday things!

During my time in charge of this ward we had 28 beds and through a year we had close to a thousand patients, so it was difficult to walk down the high street without being recognised and people wanting to talk to you. Fortunately I would be able to recognise most and what they had had done. But some mostly you had to wait and see where they were pointing to give you a clue. At one time we lived in Ruskington and one day I was walking down the high street when this lady grabbed me in a vice like grip asking 'it is Sam isn't it' when I confirmed this she went on to say that she had been waiting 9 years to thank me for looking after her husband. Fortunately he was still alive and well.

Sisters and charge nurses all went for coffee in the restaurant at the same time, so we could catch up, exchange views etc. One day going back to the ward and walking down the corridor one sister remarked 'Mrs Smith has just died' so the question was how did she know? She explained that when a big black crow lands on the sluice roof, someone dies. I found this hard to believe however she insisted I go with her to the ward and sure enough Mrs Smith had died.

In the 80s the whole running of the NHS began to change. The most significant was that 'managers' started to call the shots and every penny had to be accounted for. This type of administration saw an increase in people who never went near a patient, who commanded quite good salaries some of which were paid more than a surgeon! I think I first noticed this when I was not a Charge Nurse any more but a resource that had a cost implication. I was apparently now a manager. I drew the line when a painter was sent to inscribe my office door with the same but when I showed him a copy of my contract he said he would leave it, and he never returned. Any ward with a sister in charge was not changed either.

One the big changes that came about was a visit from the Audit Commission , where they visited all wards and departments to find out where we were spending too much money!! Or that was how we felt. One of the things they picked up on was that I and some other wards about every 6 weeks would give the permanent staff an extra half day off prior to their normal weekend off, a suitable reward for all the missed coffee breaks, lunch breaks and the many times for being late off duty. At that time the 'good will' was accepted as the norm and was neve moaned about. We were told this practice had to stop unless proof of the time owing was kept. To comply with this, sisters and charge nurses gave all staff concerned a small note book in which they would log all the time owing, this in turn had to be authenticated by the senior person on duty and always by a trained member of staff. This change showed that in fact I had to give them an extra half shift ever 4 weeks instead of every 6 as previous. After a few weeks the senior manager told us to revert to the previous system. I think this showed how the health service was supplemented by a workforce who were paid to do a job not work a given set of hours at any one time!

One of the initiatives that came out of this was that it was thought that when a patient unfortunately died on your ward it would save the ward staff some time if the family could collect the property and death certificate from the general office. We tried to argue that this interaction was part of our role not something removed from it. However the powers that be said this must be done. It took 2 weeks for the system to be changed back as the admin office could not cope with the emotion of dealing with distressed relatives and mostly had to refer them back to the ward staff anyway. Another daft decision made by someone who knew nothing of care.

The most emotive decision was to <u>save money</u> by having mixed sex wards. Anyone with any sense could see this would not work, except work against the principles of care and human dignity Again we outlined the problems which may/would arise but go ahead it must! All the problems we could for see happened but it took nearly 20 years before the situation was reversed after a long campaign by many organisations, citing the same reasons why, we had said it would not work.

So many stupid decisions made by people commanding enormous salaries who had no idea what a patients needs were. It always seemed the first consideration would always be 'how much money can we save' so that we can look good. There were some very capable managers unfortunately, they had to toe the party line. I once read that during this time there was a reduction in medical and nursing staff of about 10%. Administration staff increased by 110%. Not sure whether this was true but it sure felt like it sometimes. I am sure other professions e.g. police and teachers had the same problems.

A job was advertised for a car park manager of a large hospital in the midlands at an enormous salary for which you could get almost 2 trained nurses. One hospital had underspent their budget by a few thousand pounds and they were unable to put in the budget for the following year and it had to be returned to central funds. So instead of doing this, they bought all of the staff a bible!! Hard to believe but true.

At this time nurse training was going through a change, this initiative was called 'Project 2000' and was the forerunner of what would eventually make nurse training a degree course. I was asked to attend the interview process for the next intake of students. I must say I felt a bit out of my depth as the panel was made up of Senior tutors and their team, all of which had Degrees , PHD's etc. as the day went on it was obvious they were looking for degree material of which there was a lot to choose from. I was looking for who I thought would have good grades and yet have the ability to relate to patients at the bedside, a very basic quality and yet in my opinion was fundamentally the most important. One interviewee (who I later found out was the niece of a trained nurse who I knew very well) had good grades, interviewed well, although nervous and I considered her probably the best candidate we had seen, I felt the panel were in agreement with me, that is until one question the 'egg heads' asked was "what book are you reading at the moment" without hesitation the reply was "The latest Jackie Collins novel". This was the end of the interview. When we were in the process of reviewing all candidates, this girl was top of my pile! The other panel members all put her in the rejects pile saying 'anyone who reads that rubbish cannot do a degree 'When I got back to my ward, her auntie rang to see how she had got on, as she knew I was interviewing but didn't want to ask for any preferential treatment. I told her my thoughts and how unjust she had been treated, and suggested she should apply to Boston Pilgrim hospital as they were not as yet starting the degree course. She did and was readily accepted. About 3 years later I had the occasion to visit my Mum who was in the Pilgrim following a hip operation and who should be on this ward but the nurse I endeavoured to advice. Without even asking my Mum pointed her out as being one her favourites. When I was speaking to the ward sister about Mum's progress, I couldn't resist asking about this girl, the reply being she was one the best student nurses she had helped to train and when she qualified in 2 months' time, she was hoping to have a job for her on the permanent team. Our loss, their gain!!!

Chapter Twenty Three: OK let's have more funny stories

My ward was a nightingale style with 28 beds including a 4 bed sideward. On one occasion the intensive care unit needed some maintenance, so my side ward was commissioned to be ICU for as long as necessary. As some routine surgery needed ICU facilities, this had to be postponed as the sideward would not have the amount of facility required. There was of course emergencies which, could be managed but, fortunately on this occasion, not many.

Most of the time one bed was occupied by a 15 yrs. old girl following an RTA and was unconscious but able to breath on her own. A good friend of mine was sister in the unit and as neither of us were very busy and had time for a chat. During this time I was able to get to know the patients parents and able to find out what her likes were in music, hobbies etc. I was also pleased to find out she was, like me a big fan of Liverpool FC. The family brought in some music for her to listen to using head phones and when I was able to would talk to her about football and Liverpool in particular. One Saturday afternoon I was on late shift and during the evening was able to get in to see her. I was able to tell her that Liverpool had won. At this point she gave my hand a squeeze, opened one eye and uttered the words "did Keegan score?" Her first words for about 3 weeks. What a delightful surprise. She then began to make a steady improvement and able to go home. It was one of those situations where her parents would call in to let me know how she was getting on. She eventually started a career as a care assistant in a nursing home, and went on to get married and have a family.

We had in a young man of 25yrs. For what is known as a Pan-procto colectomy for ulcerative colitis which unfortunately had failed to respond to medical treatment. This involves the removal of all the bowel from the ileum down to and removal of the rectum and anus and the perineum closed. This means the patient is left with an ileostomy which opens on to the front of the abdomen which has to have a bag attached (I think there are advances in 20th century)

One of the complications of this type of surgery was the patient may end up impotent. On this occasion it would have been devastating for this young man who was a travelling salesman for a well-known soft drinks company. He travelled the length and breadth of the country and had a 'girlfriend' in every town. He obviously was requested to give informed consent for the operation after having all the implications explained to him. At that time we had a stoma specialist who I think probably scared the poor lad to death and he doubtfully was not going to have the surgery. Prior to the surgery I was on duty the weekend before and spent most of the time trying to keep him positive and when Monday came he was agreeing to the surgery. The recovery was uneventful and went very well. I am not sure why I took his sutures out but I did (normally a member of the team would do this or I would supervise a student as part of their training) after the suture removal I suggested he take a warm bath and then he would feel better. After about half an hour of him being soaking in the bath I heard this shouting "Sam, Sam come here quickly" Shit, I am thinking his wound has broken open!? And rushed to the bathroom and on pushing the door open I was greeted with "what do you think of this" as he laid there with a grin on his face and an enormous erection. Excellent result and for months after we were kept in the soft drinks of whatever he was selling at the time. I have recounted this true story many times. A true story of which you could not write the script.

When I first took charge of Robey there were 2 patients who had been admitted previously following horrific car or motor cycle accidents and both were in a semi-conscious state. One of which remained so until he died four and a half years later. The other young man (I will call Dave, not his real name)) began to recover and eventually went home, he was unable to work but led a happy independent life! During his prolonged recovery, which was a very slow process he passed through various stages and this manifested into very basic actions such as picking his nose, scratching, playing with himself and for some unknown reason would stick his hand up his bum and pull out any faeces that happened to be bothering him!?

   To set the scene, every Sunday afternoon there was always some religious input. On alternate weeks we would get the student priests from the local theological college, who were really good and talked to the patients, share stories etc. and it was not unknown we could have a card school! On the other weekend we had a fringe Baptist group, the leader of which was a real 'fire and brimstone 'sort of preacher who most refused to listen to and the others ignored him. They were eventually banned from coming in to the hospital for their session following one episode on my ward when the preacher said that all the patients were in hospital because they were all sinners and a number of patients and relatives complained.

Any way back to the story. The usual Sunday afternoon, all is fairly quiet and peaceful. Right on queue in comes the troop led by the minister followed by his entourage of ladies in their finery, smelling of lily of the valley, they in turn were followed by a dorky youth pushing the upright piano. So the 'service' begins with the usual jolly hymns followed by a bit of ranting and raving by the minister. So we come to the final hymn. We were sitting there wishing it all to end soon when we notice that Dave has his hand and fingers up his arse trying to evacuate a big turd. At this point we all withdraw to the kitchen but continued to observe a success with the evacuation which, when he had got a good handful promptly threw it only to land it on top of the piano. The music and singing immediately ceased and the minister looked for help but .we were nowhere to be seen. The pianist was asked by the minister to carry on with the hymn. After a few minutes the whole group promptly made an exit complete with steaming turd on the top of the piano. I suppose looking back it would today have raised all sorts of issues and maybe it was bordering on the indecent but it was extremely funny at the time. Fair justice for insisting on us all being sinners!!!

One Saturday we admitted a young man with concussion sustained when he fell off his chair during his drag act. It was summer, all his friends would come to visit and parade down the ward (a nightingale ward. 66 yards long) the patient was in the last bed on the right Invariably they wore lederhosen and camped up the parade with style though, this did raise a few eyebrows amongst the patients In the opposite bed to him on he left was 35/40year old who had had his appendix out 3 days before and was recovering well. A nurse was talking to him and asked if he was ok, the reply being he had belly ache due to trapped wind. The nurse explained to him this was normal after this operation due to bowel being sluggish because handling of the bowel during the operation and had a name 'paralytic ileus' and that he would feel better when he had passed wind, Immediately he responded that he daren't fart in case the guy in the bed opposite thought he was blowing him a kiss. Fortunately the young man was discharged later that day and appendectomy chap was able to rip a few off and recovered very quickly. This was the early 70's so we have to be aware of political incorrectness at that time.

Chapter twenty Four: Christmas time

Christmas was always special. I think I probably had no more than about 5 Christmas's off in all my career, but this was not unusual as all sisters and charge nurses were expected to be there on Christmas day.

With regards to off/on duty it was essential to cover the Christmas/New year's eve period with adequate numbers of staff and skill mix. To make it fair all round about 6 weeks prior to the festive season I would give the staff an on duty rota to fill in with their requests and say they must negotiate and agree with each other until all the criteria for cover was met and everyone was happy. This way we always had the needs of the ward fulfilled, and everyone got what they wanted off.

We were not allowed to have many decorations and only have them up until Boxing Day. Christmas day was a vote to show a best decorated ward. It did depend how soon you started to plan them and then how busy you were to be able to put them up, so keep it minimalist if you can, or as one year I had had a head teacher of a local primary school in for surgery about 6 weeks before Christmas. He called in one day for a chat and during the conversation the decorating subject came up and he said he would get all of his children to make a collage about 6x4 feet depicting different Christmas carols and we could put one on the blank wall above every bed. 2 days before Christmas he arrived with about 10 children and hung the collages as promised. In the evening when it got dark we turned the bed head lights upside down (unless the patients needed them) and then put the main ward lights out, the ward looked like a church with stained glass windows. That year we won 1st, prize of an extra mince pie and glass off Matrons punch!!

Leading up to this all the wards would have identified the consultants who would be in fancy dress identifying a theme. Again this was a competition. The chosen consultant would also be responsible for carving the turkey, surgeons having a distinct advantage! After the turkey carving and all patients had eaten their dinner and presents were given to each patient. The consultants would then visit all of the other wards and eventually finish in the consultants lounge where Matron was host for her infamous punch and nibbles. Most consultants and their teams were by this time fairly pissed. It was wonderful to see them with their families enjoying the fun but they were always respected the next day. One year our ward had a theme of ancient Rome, ENT consultant was Mark Antony, his houseman was Caesar but best of all the maxilla-facial consultant was Cleopatra and was so well made up that his family did not recognise him. All wards took part and some of the costumes were really outstanding. Eventually this tradition began to wane when money became an issue, we used to get a turkey for each ward irrespective of how many patients you had in, and thus part of the celebration was the carving ceremony. As time went on if you had 6 patients, the kitchen would send 6 slices of turkey already plated up. Subsequently this tradition and most enjoyable time sadly came to an end.

Christmas Eve was always celebrated with a carol service by all the staff. Nurses taking part would always be wearing uniform with their capes turned inside out so they looked bright red, carrying lanterns, a truly spectacular sight. This was always accompanied by the hospital brass band or the local Salvation Army brass band. One year we had a young guy who had had his catheter removed 2 days before Christmas Eve, although he had regained full control he didn't feel confident to leave his urinal very far away. So all the patients who were able were taken out to the corridor where the band was playing. This young man was getting carried away and lifting his hands in time with beat forgetting he had his urinal in his hand which; was half full of pee Some of the contents shot out and unfortunately landed in the top of the poor bandsman's euphonium. Oh dear. Very embarrassing.One other tradition was the Sister or Charge Nurse on each ward was to cook full English breakfast for all the staff and patients if they were allowed. This was until the powers that be decided we did not need a cooker anymore and gave us a microwave instead. We were able to get round this by bringing in a camping stove and thus able to fulfil the tradition.

Chapter Twenty six: Reflections!

I never did not want to go to work. In all professions there is usually a saying that we lived through the best times, we have all heard the saying 'not in my day'. I have witnessed so many changes in my long career, some good, and some bad but, through all of this I do belief that in the nursing profession the basic qualities and commitment to caring remain as strong as ever in 2021 and for that reason, we all live in the best period whatever time we are in.

In recent months I have had to avail myself of the nursing profession and other members of the multidisciplinary team that make up care in the 21st century at Lincoln County Hospital.

I must say I have been amazed at the quality of personal care I have received. All this through this awful Coronavirus pandemic. I am pleased to say the standards of nursing are as high as they have always been and I remain very proud to have been a part of the Lincoln County Hospital history.

Acknowledgements

I obviously have met an awful lot of people in my career and it would be impossible to remember them all however, here are a selection who I especially remember with admiration.

From my time at St Johns.

Chris Poynton(CMN), Jack Broughton(Senior Tutor), Larry Winterbottom(Tutor), Cliff Kilmister, Grenville Longdon, Noel Twigg, Noel Rogers, Ray Rodgers, Bill Carrott,Ken Jackson, Brian King, Janko Benner, Tony Saenz-Sanchez, Derek Willoughby, Bill Mathers, Eddie Baker, Arthur Wells, Dave McFall, Bill Dales, Dick Taff, Alan Grinnell, Vince Towriss, Norman Taylor, Tom Halpin, Alf Briggs, Paul Hyde, Jim Woodburn, George Creasey, Miss McNulty(Matron)

I wish to acknowledge nurses everywhere, particularly those to whom I have the utmost respect and thank them for their support and help throughout my career. There are too many to mention as individuals but I am sure you know who you are, though a special mention of the Robey rebels must be made. I am not really sure where this label came from though I think it was one of the trained staff. Over the years there inevitably were many changes in the team but most stayed for a very long time and are remembered with affection. Thank you one and all, you made my life extremely happy and proud.

Starting at October 1970

There were Pam Pacey, Francis Carnell, Hilda Shaw (who was 81 yrs. when she retired) Sue Ranson, Jan Nye, Moya Blea, Patsy Wright, Jill Stanger, Kath Howie, Bet Kunzle, Jean McLean, Eileen Curtis, Kim Shucksmith, Della Kime, Janet Castleton, Sylvia Wilkinson, Kim Gabbitas, Fiona Howie. Then there were the domestic team Mary, Joan and many more, the names evade me but I remember their faces extremely well.

Not to forget: Miss Winifred Parker (Matron), Miss Snowdon Assistant matron. Elizabeth Lovely(tutor), Miss J Ibbotson(tutor)Jean McLaren(Mack), Kath Blood, Gran Danby, Pat Harrington, John Goddard, Colin Raby, Olive Millar, Pippa Pick, Jo Kime, Maureen Saffin, Chris Couling. Also remembered with much admiration the many skilful, brilliant surgeons I had the pleasure to work with

There are also many people in all other departments in a hospital porters, admin, laborities, laundry dept., kitchen and all the artisans, without them we would not function I am sure I have failed to mention some, which is not my intention and I apologise for missing anyone

■■i